♥ ♥ ♥

The Little Bo

MW00571178

Online Romance

How to Find It ♥ How to Keep it

Lorilyn Bailey

L♦O♦R♦M♦A♦X
Communications

Raleigh, North Carolina
United States of America

www.online-romance.com

♥ ♥ ♥

The Little Book of Online Romance

♥

♥

ISBN 0-9641239-6-7

Published in the United States of America by

LORMAX Communications, PO Box 40304, Raleigh, NC 27629-0304

Note: This book is sold primarily for use as entertainment; the publisher and author are not engaged in rendering professional marriage counseling or advice. If expert assistance is required, seek the services of a qualified professional.

Table of Contents

♥ ♥ ♥

Can You Find True Romance On This Thing?
by Guy McCool

Can you find true romance on this thing?
Does Cyberspace love exist?
And if you found a perfect love...
how would you be kissed?

Can modems send skipped heartbeats...
to show the way you feel?
Or will the passion that you send...
appear to be unreal?

And what about your heartfelt gaze?
Will it be betrayed?
When a JPEG file is opened...
and your image is displayed?

Can you find true romance on this thing?
Should you love without regret?
And if by chance, you should fall...
will you be saved by the Internet?

Will your email messages....
seem like Valentines...

And will you feel your lover's intent...
when you read between the lines?

Can love be sustained with keyboard strokes
and gentle clicks of mice?
Or will online romantics end up,
seeking forlorn lover's advice?

Can you find true romance on this thing?
Elusive as it seems...
Or should you keep true love confined...
to secret, ethereal dreams?

Is love too precious for technical realms,
completely out of place?
Does it require its own private world...
outside of Cyberspace?

Is AOL the place to search for love?
I haven't got a clue.
I guess when all is said and done...
the choice is up to you!

Introduction: Is Online Romance Possible?

Online romance. What is it? Is it a great new way of meeting new people? Or is it a waste of time and a sure way to get your heart broken? Guy McCool eloquently posed this question, in a poem, on the previous page. (Feel free to sing his poem to the tune of your favorite country/western song.)

Online services and the Web can be wonderful introductory tools—better than your own personal matchmaker. It's fun to meet people online who share your interests. If, by chance, you meet someone you find interesting, and the feeling is mutual, that's a great way to start off a relationship! However, you must learn to navigate the waters, to watch for sharks, and to steer clear of other dangers. You must remember that when you think you caught the "big one," you may find that your hook is imbedded, instead, in nothing more than an old shoe, caked with seaweed—bearing no resemblance to the great catch you were imagining. Remember, too, there are always other fish in the sea.

There are plenty of stories of people who have met online, carried on a long-distance relationship, met each other, been disappointed, broken up, and swore

never to go near a computer again! Yet there are others who have found their soulmates, married, and live happy and fulfilling lives.

So does seeking love online work or doesn't it? As in real life, meeting your true love in cyperspace has a lot to do with what you do, where you go, and whether or not you stumble upon a good healthy dose of good luck. *Yet online romance offers unique benefits (as well as some pitfalls).*

In this little book, I'll help you learn what to do and where to go, as well as what to ask when you find someone you'd like to know better. As in life, there are no guarantees; but you will be well equipped to begin your cyberspace adventure.

I wish you the best of luck in your quest!

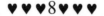

What's the Web?

Before the Web was developed, text-based options used for communication and research purposes (mailing lists, Usenet, Gopher, FTPs) made up the Internet, which is the planet's largest network of computer networks.

The Web is the part of the Internet that is easy to use and to understand, and it's the most fun. You can click on a word with your mouse and "travel" all over the planet! Today, the terms "Web" or "Net" are often used to describe the entire Internet system.

A Very, Very Brief History of the Web

If you are ever at a party, and someone asks, "Hey, how did the Web start, anyway?" you will be able to answer, because you would have read the following simplified version of its history. (Skip it if you don't want to appear educated.)

- In 1945, Vannevar Bush wrote about the concept of hypertext and hoped his "Memex machine" would help people handle the increasing amount of data in the world. (Perhaps you can name your first child, "Vannevar.")

♥ ♥ ♥

- In the late sixties, a U.S. Department of Defense project linked the defense department, military research contractors, and universities. This connected system of computers grew and grew. And grew. And grew some more.

- In the early eighties, Ted Nelson wrote a book and used the word "hypertext" (relating to documents linked by text). Tim Berners-Lee, a scientist in Switzerland, used the term "Web" to describe his idea of linking data.

- In the late eighties, Hypercard, the first hypertext computer application, became available for use with the Macintosh computer. (Those were the glory days.) Berners-Lee also began working with Robert Calliau to develop hypertext.

- In the late eighties and early nineties, America Online, Prodigy, and Compuserve were developed.

- In May of 1991 (not that long ago!), the World Wide Web was announced on Usenet, the global system of discussion groups.

- In 1993, Marc Andreesen released a program called Mosaic, which allowed users to use windows, scroll bars, clicks, and so on, to view the Web. Mosaic is called a "browser." Mosaic made it easier to view the Web.

- Soon after, Andreesen left Mosaic and developed Netscape, an improvement over Mosaic. Netscape stock went bananas, and those involved became very wealthy very quickly. The majority of Internet users now use Netscape. Bill Gates' Internet Explorer is gaining speed.

- In the nineties, Internet Service Providers (ISPs), companies that provide email capability and Web access proliferated. *Thereafter, the world went nuts.*

♥ ♥ ♥

What You Need to Start

In order to begin your adventure, you need an IBM-compatible computer (*duh*), (at least a 386; preferably a 486 or better, with 4 megabytes of memory, running Windows 3.1 or higher) or a Macintosh. If you can afford it, buy a new, not a used, computer. A new one will be equipped to handle the features you'll most likely want in the near future. You also need a modem, and a telephone line that does not have a Call Waiting feature on it.

If you bought a new computer in 1995 or later, you have it made. You really have it made if the new computer has an internal modem already installed (it probably does). If you have an older computer and you need a modem or you want one faster than the one you have, you can buy an external or internal modem and install it or have someone install it.

Check local office-supply stores for modems; you may find your best bet is buying it by mail. You might try A+ Computer at (800) 505-7400 for modems and other computer parts. They have good prices on good products and were very nice to me when I upgraded to a faster modem.

♥ ♥ ♥

Make sure your modem speed is at least at 14400 kilobits per second (bps) speed, preferably 28800. The higher your modem speed, the faster the text and graphics will appear on the screen when you are on the Web or using an online service. If you have an older modem with a speed of 2400 or 9600, you will end up beating your computer with your fists as you wait forever for the graphics to appear.

...Okay, we have that out of the way! No more of that techie stuff for the rest of the book. Promise.

♥ ♥ ♥

Methods of Cyberspace Communication

There are several ways for you to get to know other people in cyberspace. Generally, you need to either subscribe to a commercial online service or subscribe to an Internet service provider (ISP). Within these services, you have many options.

Commercial Online Services

Commercial online services, such as America Online (AOL), offer the following resources:

- Chat rooms
- Message Boards
- Email
- Online Events
- Internet Access

♥ ♥ ♥

The Internet

You can access the Internet through a commercial online service or through an Internet Service Provider (ISP). (More on those later.)

The Internet is the most amazing, extraordinary, awesome, astonishing, and remarkable phenomenon and is sure to affect our lives in wondrous ways for many years.

The World Wide Web is the part of the Internet that handles multimedia (text, graphics, audio, animation, and video). You use browser software (such as Netscape, Mosaic, or Internet Explorer) to view the documents. (By the way, you don't have to purchase these programs; your online service provider offers one as part of their service, or you can download them [copy them to your computer] from the Web for free.)

Businesses, educational institutions, governments, assorted organizations, and independent individuals from around the world create web documents using a language called HTML, or HyperText Markup Language. HTML uses tags to indicate such elements as new paragraphs, bold text, and text that is linked to other web pages. <p>This sentence is written in HTML</p>.

♥ ♥ ♥

When you use your mouse to click on linked text (usually blue-color text), the document to which that text is linked appears on your screen. By clicking on those links, you have access to millions of documents on millions of subjects from around the world.

The Web is entertainment, education, research, advertising, and communication. It's a bookstore, a mall, a library, a university, a cafe, a post office, an arcade, a TV, a dating service, a medical center, and thousands of other resources all wrapped into one—delivered to your computer for your viewing pleasure.

You can spend a few lifetimes surfing the Web, and you'd still never see it all. If you haven't yet "surfed the Web," try it, you'll love it.

The most incredible thing about the Internet is that all the computers linked to the Web are, in essence, linked to each other. All of those computers have people sitting in front of them, surfing, creating, learning, doing business, having fun. *One of those computer users is looking for YOU.*

The Internet has the following resources for meeting others:

Commercial and Private Web Sites

- ### Matchmaking Services (profit and non-profit)

Because the Internet is a new medium, hundreds of matchmaking services and personal ad businesses have recently popped up. Unfortunately, the operators of these businesses often do not have the equipment to operate the service properly, or the web site is not designed very well.

Before you sign up for a matchmaking service, make sure you know all the charges. Some are 100% free, while some are free to the person who places the ad, but anyone who responds to your ad must use a 900-number to get more information. Others are offered by subscription for a certain number of hours spent viewing the web site.

Spend some time looking at the matchmaking services listed in the back of the book. Take advantage of any free trial.

If you decide to place an ad, word it carefully. Do not give any personal identifying information, such as real name, address, or phone number. Some services offer anonymous email addresses, which is a good idea.

Tip:
Use a search engine (more on this later) to look for your city's **online** newspaper, if it has one.
Check out its "Personals" section.

- **Chat Rooms**

    Many commercial Internet sites now have chat rooms that are easy to get into and to chat with whomever pops in to say hello. Chat rooms are web sites in which two or more people can write text on the screen, and anyone who has entered the site can read the text. These commercial Internet (non-AOL) chat sites are usually not conducive to romance, but you may wish to explore them anyway, just for fun. Most of the time, you can't tell who has logged into the room.

    Chat rooms in commercial online services, such as America Online, on the other hand, provide (in the upper right hand corner of the "room") a list of screen names of anyone who has entered the room. You may also access a "private room" if you wish.

Remember that anything you type is probably being logged somewhere or is being read by lurkers. Lurkers are people who may watch an online discussion but not participate. You should do a lot of lurking at first so you know what's going on.

If you'd like to start up a conversation with people from around the planet, check out these Internet sites:

Emporium's Chat Links
http://www.www.webcom.com/fi/empo.htm/
More than 350 chat links

Webchat Broadcasting System (WBS)
http://www.irsociety.com/wbs.html
Chat. Nice graphics.

Sol Chat-O-Rama
http://www.solscape.com/chat/
Hundreds of chat links.

- **Internet Telephone/Web Video Conferencing**

  The future is here! You can actually talk to someone over the Internet if you and your sweetie have the right software and hardware (and bypass the phone company!).

  * Take a look at **http://www.freetel.com.** This is a free service, supported by advertising, that allows you to speak to loved ones, or anyone, around the world for *free*. You need standard computer equipment, a sound card, and a microphone. Check it out!

  If you obtain the appropriate video camera and software, you can get an eyeful of the person you're emailing.

  For information on telephones that work via the Internet and through your computer, see:
  http://www.www.emagic.com/
  http://www.von.com

  For internet telephone and video conferencing information:
  http://www.vocaltec.com/

  Internet Phone Directory (for people who can access voice messages)
  http://www.pulver.com/iphone/

♥ ♥ ♥

- **Usenet**

  Usenet is a vast system of discussion groups (called "newsgroups") on a vast variety of subjects. The discussions are created by email messages that are posted in one spot that anyone interested can access, and anyone can post responses.

  For more information on Usenets, see a list of Usenet FAQs (FrequentlyAsked Questions) at **http://www.cis.ohio-state.edu/ hypertext/faq/ usenet.** You can also view and subscribe to Usenet discussion groups from: **http://www.search.com/**. To look for newsgroups in your area, start looking through those listed at **http://www.tilenet.com**.

  Some Usenet discussion groups that may interest you:

  alt.romance
  alt.romance.chat
  alt.romance.mature-adult
  alt.romance.online
  alt.weddings
  alt.personals.ads (this is the only one in this list for posting ads;
      the others are for *discussions* only.)

- **Mailing Lists**

  Mailing lists (also called listservs) consist of discussions and information by email on all types of subjects. You subscribe to a list and receive all the messages that other subscribers have "posted" (sent). As a subscriber, you can also post messages that all subscribers will receive in their email inboxes. Mailing lists are by subscription (free, of course) and usually reach much smaller groups than Usenet newsgroups. See **http://www.tile.net/tile/listserv/index.html.**

  To subscribe, you send an email message to the administrative address of the list. Generally, you type the word "subscribe," then the name of the list, and then your first and last names. When you want to post a message to the group, you send it to another address. Many Usenet newsgroups have mailing lists.

  Mailing lists can be a lot of fun; you can meet a whole group of people who are interested in the same things that you are. I belong to a book-related group, and it's like having 400 friendly penpals.

- **Internet Relay Chat**

Internet Relay Chat (IRC) is similar to America Online chat rooms, without the fancy graphics or ease of use. (If you have an Internet Service Provider [ISP] plan with one monthly fee for unlimited Internet usage, however, you may save a lot of money!) You need IRC software, which is available at **http://cws. wilmington. net/irc.html** for Windows. For Mac users, go to **ftp://cs-ftp .bu.edu/irc/ clients/macintosh/.** When you connect, you get a list of IRC channels that you can join. Some that may interest you include: #romance, #affairs, and #35plus. (It's free, of course.) Give it a try.

Bulletin Board Services

Bulletin Board Services (BBSs) are like small online services. There are BBSs run by computer companies that provide technical support. Others are run by single individuals, for profit or for fun. There are thousands and thousands of BBSs around the world, with chat groups that discuss thousands of topics. You'll find the greatest variety of them in large cities. BBSs may or may not be linked to the Web.

How to find a BBS? Ask your nerdy friends or relatives, or look at the latest computer magazines. Of course, you can also review BBS lists on the Web at **http://www.dkeep.com/sbi.html** to see if any are of interest to you. (You'll find that everything on earth seems to be on the Web.)

You usually need to find a BBS in your area because when your computer modem dials into their system, you want it to be a local (free) telephone call. However, at least one Internet Service Provider, BBS Direct, 1-800-939-4262, offers local telephone access to 35 of the top BBSs in the country along with its other services. Of course, you still have to abide by any of the rules or fees from any one of those BBSs. BBSs are not as easy to use as AOL; but once you get online, it's fun.

Email

You can communicate by email with anyone in the world who has an email address. (No long-distance telephone charges or post office charges apply!)

Muds

Muds are games played by many people (with great imaginations) in imaginary environments. For more information, check out the FAQ (a list of frequently asked questions) at **http://wwww.cis.ohio-state.edu/hypertext/faw/usenet/games/mud-faq/top.html.**

ImagiNation Network, a subscription service from AT&T, **http://www.att. com/truechoice/imagra2.html,** is also a place where many couples have met while playing online games. Another fun site (this one free) is **http://www. thepalace.com**, which has a great selection of virtual reality chat rooms.

Commercial Online Services

America Online (AOL), CompuServe, and Prodigy are commercial online services.

When you install AOL , CompuServe, or Prodigy (free) computer disks in your computer, (and share your charge card number with them) you can take advantage of all types of fun services and information resources they offer, such as chat rooms, clubs, interest groups, magazines, bulletin boards, and even workshops and on-line courses. These services are available to you only by subscription; that

subscription includes access to the entire Internet. You can also send and receive email messages to anyone in the world, whether or not they are AOL subscribers.

Tip:
If you receive an official-looking request from AOL via email or an instant message requesting your charge number or password because there is some problem with it, ignore it!

AOL never asks for your password and asks for your charge card number just once when you first sign up. The people asking you for that information after you've signed up are hackers. They steal your password, use your online time, and charge it to your charge card...and who knows what else.

America Online is the largest commercial online service with more than 6 million subscribers. CompuServe has more than 4 million members. Prodigy, on the other hand, has a mere 1.5 million members and isn't growing as fast as AOL.

Each service provides unique services and has its own "culture." America Online is engaging, friendly, and easy to use. Prodigy is family oriented and has many options for singles to meet. CompuServe is targeted toward business types and has limited resources for those seeking online romance. However, as you may have heard, Rush Limbaugh did find his match there. That's reason enough for me to advise you to try another service.

America Online, CompuServe, and Prodigy all offer free software and a free trial period. Order them all, and take advantage of the free time. Make sure you use them one at a time. If you don't have enough space on your hard drive, you may muck everything up by loading them all at once. When you have completed the trial period of one service, delete its files before you load another service. Then decide which one you'll keep.

The world of the Web and online services is constantly changing. Prices and services continue to fluctuate. Nearly all of the online services (in addition to the "Big 3") provide free software and trial periods, so don't be afraid to experiment once you get the hang of it.

As competition heats up, all online services are offering better deals for consumers. For the latest offers, or to order the free software, call the numbers located in "Resources" in the back of the book. Usually, the cost involves some type of base monthly charge for a certain number of hours, with extra charges for each additional hour.

In this little book, I focus on America Online, because it is the easiest, quickest way you can go online and meet people. Much of the information, however, applies to any of the services.

Internet Service Providers

Internet Service Providers, also known as ISPs, are different from commercial online services. ISPs often provide only email service and Internet access. Usually (but not always) ISPs offer service to a limited region.

ISPs are a great deal, because in some areas, fees are as low as $8 to $25 a month. That means you can send messages to anyone in the world who has an email address, and you can play on the Web for hours, for no extra hourly fees. As with the commercial online services, competition will drive down prices.

When deciding on a service, you must find out whether the access number used (the number that your modem will automatically dial once you log in) is a long distance number. If so, you will pay long-distance charges every time you're online. (Not a good thing. You need a local access number.)

♥ ♥ ♥

To find an ISP in your area, you can either ask your friends or relatives for suggestions, or once you're on the Internet through AOL, look up this address: **http://www.thelist.com/**. There, listed by state, and by area codes, are ISPs. When you find one in your town, call and ask about their most cost-effective plans, and ask about technical support, too. When things go wrong, you will want to talk to someone about it as soon as possible. As the Web has boomed, so have ISPs; some are better than others. You definitely want 24-hour, toll-free, technical support.

It's easier if the ISP has a software disk you can use to load the program; some programs with no disks are confusing to start up. To begin, simply follow the instructions on the disk. If you're the least bit apprehensive about it, invite a friend over who already has an online service.

If you generally do not use the minimum number of hours offered per month on America Online, you do not need to subscribe to an ISP. If you go over that minimum, it might be a good idea to start comparing services and prices.

I have an ISP as well as AOL. I keep AOL because I enjoy its chat rooms, but I also like the unlimited email time and unlimited Internet access provided by my ISP for one low monthly price. When you begin to "surf the Web" you will most likely want to leisurely explore new and exciting sites. Check out the costs of all the online services to determine which one is the best choice for your viewing habits.

Phone companies have joined the Web party; AT&T, MCI, and Sprint all offer online service connections. Take a look at what they offer, too. Phone numbers are on Page 148.

♥ ♥ ♥

Etiquette of the Net

Using email is a whole new way to communicate. It's a bit of a cross between casual conversation and written notes. The inflections in your voice and the look in your eye are missing in this medium, so you have to be more careful in communicating your message.

Follow these basic rules when you use email or you are in chat rooms:

- **Be careful with your wording.** Use emoticons (also known as "smileys,") to enhance your online correspondence. Be careful with sarcasm; your words may appear to the reader to be a cruel joke instead of a witty remark. An emoticon can soften your words. This is an emoticon: :-)   (Look sideways to see it.) You'll find a list of emoticons on Page 140.

- **Avoid being wordy in an email.** It takes some people longer to download email messages than it does others. Also, if people are paying for access by the hour, they don't want to spend it all downloading your one long wordy thought.

- **Fill in the subject line** of your email message. Make it easy for your reader to glance at your message in his or her "incoming" list and to determine its content.

- **Treat everyone nicely.** Don't send nasty little notes (called flames). Also, don't assume that someone is flaming you; it's easy to misinterpret information online.

- **Use acronyms (shortcuts) when appropriate** and when you know your reader understands them. You'll find a list of acronyms on Page 142. The following is an example of acronym over-use:

  "BTW, FWIW, before you asked that question, I think you should have RTFM. WRT that question, it was so goofy, it made me ROTFL."

Translation: *"By the way, for what it's worth, I think you should read the freakin' manual. With respect to that question, it was so goofy, it made me roll on the floor, laughing."*

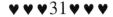

♥ ♥ ♥

- **Never send an email when you are angry.** Email messages are easy to cut and paste and forward to someone else (or to several people at once), so they may backfire on you. If you feel compelled to reply in anger, wait 24 hours, and then craft a brief, carefully worded response reeking with sarcasm, such as, "Yeah, right. Whatever." If you're still angry after 24 hours, seek professional help. Or you may just need a vacation.

- **Do not type in caps**, LIKE THIS, because it is considered shouting. It is irritating to others and is a clue to everyone that you are a newcomer (otherwise known as a "newbie") to the Web. Of course, sometimes, YOU JUST FEEL LIKE SHOUTING. I KNOW I DO.

- **Lurk a little.** When you "enter" a chat room, or subscribe to a newsgroup, watch what is going on before commenting. Get the feel of the room. Every established group of people anywhere has its own little customs and rules. In some chat rooms, people may speak one at a time; you'll get flamed for interrupting. In others, everyone types at once, so there will be many conversations taking place at once—like a big party.

♥ ♥ ♥

- **Don't jump into a chat room and ask for an "age/sex/location" check.** It's like jumping into someone's face, in real life, and asking, "How old are you? Are you a guy or a girl? Where are you?" (It's rather rude.) Some chat rooms have banned such checks. I know I never respond to them. You don't have to, either. (But then again, if that is the "culture" of the room, go ahead and ask if you want.)

- **Don't send anyone a large file** (such as graphics, audio, video, or lot of text) without permission. Your reader may not have the system space to download such a file, and the file could muck up his whole system.

For more information on netiquette, take a look at Arlene Rinaldi's site on the web at **http://rs6000.adm.fau.edu/rinaldi/netiquette.html.**

By the way, when you enter an America Online chat room, you will see that an "Online Host" announces each member's arrival and departure. That particular host is computer generated (not a real person), so don't be angry when it doesn't answer your questions. :)

♥ ♥ ♥

Tip:

Don't use your computer at work for personal romance seeking. Some companies have systems in place that can track Web sites you visit and the times you visited them. Don't ever send anyone any email that you wouldn't mind seeing posted on the employee bulletin board. If you ever meet and fall in love with someone at your workplace, don't email personal messages to your sweetie. Company email is not personal mail; it belongs to your company.

---

cathy®

by Cathy Guisewite

The Easiest Way to Start Meeting People Online

As you now know, you can meet people online in many ways. Some are easier than others. My favorite, as you may have guessed, is America Online (AOL). Officially, AOL recommends that you do not meet in real life anyone that you met online. However, the service does provide plenty of useful resources to meet people to begin friendships.

America Online Chat Rooms

Once you install AOL in your machine, and you have selected a screen name...

Wait! First read the tip about selecting a screen name!

> **Tip:**
> *Selecting a Screen Name*
> If you select a female-sounding name, you will get a lot of attention (harassment) when you enter some chat rooms. If you pick a gender-neutral name, you will probably not be bothered.
> Be creative in deciding your name; don't accept the one that is offered to you; put some effort into creating a suitable name. It's important. After all, this will be your identity as you explore AOL. If you have trouble with the name, though, you can select another one. You can use up to five different screen names.

Okay, back to exploring AOL. If I were you, the first thing I would do after signing up is go to the main menu selection, "INTERNET CONNECTION" and when the screen pops up, select "File," then choose "Open Location." In the box, type: **http://www.thelist.com/** As I mentioned previously, that will get you to a list of Internet Service Providers (ISPs) in your area. Find the ISPs in your area code, and print the document for later use.

Now choose "Open Location" again and type: **http://wwwl.search.com/** This will get you to a great page of search engines. Search engines are simply programs

♥ ♥ ♥

in which you can type in a word or words, and the program will search the Internet for related sites. This particular site has a collection of several search engines all in one spot.

On AOL, if you select the icon with the heart; the web site address will be saved, or "bookmarked" as a "Favorite Place," and next time you can select the heart to quickly return to that site. On browsers used on the Internet, this list of favorite web sites is called a "hot list" or "bookmarks."

Just for fun, type your name into one of the Internet search engines and see what pops up. Or type in your hobby, or my name, or anything you'd like. You will get a list of web site locations; simply click on one that looks interesting, and have fun! (You're surfin' now!)

When you're finished playing, select "Back" button to go back to the main menu. Keep going back until you get to the Main Menu. (OR a much better idea is to select "GO" from the top menu bar. You'll find a window history—a list of the sites you have visited. You can select any one of those instead of repeatedly pressing "Back.")

Now you're back at the Main Menu. Two great places to find people are: "People Connection" and "Life, Styles & Interests."

People Connection

When you select "People Connection," you will be popped into a Lobby. If you're lucky, the people will be nice to you. Beware of everyone. A lot of younger people (teens, kids) visit these rooms. Watch the conversation as it unfolds in front of you. The "public" lobbies are not the best places to meet people; but you can practice your "chat room" skills here. Don't be discouraged by the childish conversation. It's better in other areas of AOL.

In a box in the upper right hand corner is a list of everyone in the room. You can double click on a name, and a dialog box pops up. You have three options:

1. If you want to know more about that person, select "Get Info." If the person created a "profile," then you will see that profile, with personal information such as name, birthday, occupation, hobbies, and interests. All this information is optional. Don't believe everything you read. (That's probably not the real Brad Pitt in the room with you.)

   By the way, you should create your own profile when you have a chance. If you have a profile, people will be more likely to strike up a conversation with you. Don't be too specific with real names or locations.

♥ ♥ ♥

2. You can select "Send Message" and you can send that person a message that no one else in the room will see. (This is called an "instant message" or an "IM.") When that person replies to you, you'll hear a little bell or noise indicating you have a response. To obtain the reply, select "Windows" and look for the person's screen name at the bottom of the list, with a checkmark next to it. Click on it and read the messages; you can communicate this way a few sentences at a time.

3. If the person is being vulgar or irritating, you can select "Ignore" and you will no longer see this person's comments. The "Ignore" feature comes in pretty handy.

Tip:
You can also find people you may know by using the Member Directory on AOL. You can search for them by typing in their names, or parts of their names, and see what pops up.

After you watch a few "Lobby" rooms in AOL, you are ready to specialize. At the top of the Lobby page are various selections. Click on "List Rooms." You'll see a list of rooms and the number of people in the rooms. Click on any one that looks interesting. Or go back to an earlier menu and explore the sites.

♥ ♥ ♥

Another option is to select "Private Room." This is where you can create a room with a name of your choosing. If others know the name, they can join you in the room. If you try the typical sex-related terms as private room names, you'll most likely find people being vulgar in those rooms. Many of them appear to be teenage boys looking for a good time. Their parents think they're doing homework. ("Wanna cyber?" they'll pant at you.) Get out while you can. It's better to ignore vulgar messages. (Unless, of course, you want to play their game. But you have a reputation to uphold, don't you? ...don't you?)

Also try typing in the name of your city or state after you select "Private Room." Later you'll read how successful this tactic was for some couples.

If you are in a public chat room, and someone is bothering you or violating the "Terms of Service" (TOS), the rules of AOL, then select Keyword and type: Guide Pager. Fill out the form, and an AOL guide may come to your rescue to handle the offender.

Many of the public rooms have AOL-provided hosts. They welcome people to the room, answer questions, keep the conversation rolling, and maintain peace.

AOL has been criticized for having these guides because some say its members are denied freedom of speech. However, I have found guides quite helpful in

handling members who act like jerks. The ones I've met are pleasant to have around. The rules are simple; if you behave, there are no problems. There are plenty of places in AOL and on the Web where you can be as vulgar as you wanna be. There are no guides, however, on the Web. (No one owns the Web.)

Another thing to be aware of in a chat room: Every word you type may be being logged as a text file, by anyone, for any reason. If you go to your menu bar and select "File" and then "Logging," you can open and name a file that will log all the comments on the chat screen until you close the file or log off AOL.

Typing one's words in a public chat room often feels as freeing as using a telephone, but your words may come back to haunt you. I've never heard of anyone who had any bad experience with having words immortalized on a logged chat, but keep in mind that some subjects you write about you may not want repeated or reread.

It is also very easy to select text and copy it to a file or email it anywhere. You may want to be careful about what you say. It is better to use email if you wish to communicate with someone on a slightly more personal basis.

Life, Styles & Interests

This is THE place to look for fun. Review the extensive list of clubs and interests and check any one that looks interesting to you. Look for any listing with "Chat" in it. You'll find that some chat rooms are empty, and others are full. Some have scheduled chats; some are open all the time.

The personalities of the rooms are quite varied; in the Military chat rooms, you'll often find veterans, and when there are scheduled "events," there are strict rules for behavior.

In the Scuba room, you'll find outdoorsy types. In the Writers' Club, you'll find journalists, novelists, and poets. In the Seniors room, you'll find a wonderful group of retirees, many from Florida. It's like visiting Mom and Dad.

There are many rooms; find one that matches your interests. Become a "regular," and get to know the other regulars. Take it slow and easy. Check profiles to see if someone is single. But don't believe everything you read. Make friends.

Relationships first built on friendships are the best kinds of relationships.

Romance-related AOL Sites

Romance Connection

Here you'll find a great resource for singles. Take a look at the Romance Connection message boards to see what people are saying about online romance. Open the files marked, "We did it!" or "Beware!" to learn about others' experiences.

This area also provides you with an opportunity to post or reply to personal ads. You can select any geographic area and read ads from people who are seeking online romance. (Keep away from those swingers.)

One of the first rules of online romance is: "Never fall in love with anyone who lives more than a tank of gas away!" That's just a joke, of course, but you might as well limit your search to your geographic area. However, that, too, can cause problems. If you live in a small town that thrives on gossip, you may want to broaden your search.

A few notes on creating personal ads: I think it is better to be very specific about what you are looking for. Read the questions in the back of this book and identify those traits that are important to you, and briefly list them to use as you

create your ad. If you cannot tolerate smoking, for example, you should mention that. Also be honest about yourself. If you deceive someone, the truth will eventually reveal itself. Honesty is good. One member described herself as "cute and chubby" and found the love of her life.

I think you might as well be somewhat wordy in these ads. You're not paying by the word as in newspaper ads. Why abbreviate? Be friendly, list your hobbies and interests. But don't share too much personal information. NEVER post your telephone number anywhere in cyberspace. In fact, if it doesn't matter one way or another to you, it's a good idea to get an unlisted phone number.

ABC Love Online

You'll find more message boards, links, and advice on online as well as "offline" relationships.

Love@aol

Among the features of Love@aol: "Steamy Message Boards," "Hot Chats, and "Tips to 'Score' Offline." I popped into the chat room and found two female hosts

pretending to kiss and snuggle up to everyone. All innocent fun, I guess. I found it rather strange that so much time was spent on so little meaningful communication.

One of the nights I visited, there were 48 people, which is quite a few for a chat room. Not that many people were chatting. Most seemed to be lurking.

Another popular area is the Message Boards. Here, you can place ads according to profession, interests, or looks.

Net Girl

According to NetGirl's host, computer journalist Rosalind Resnick, "The goal of the NetGirl Forum is to help members successfully cope with cyberlove and online relationships, both on America Online and on the Internet, and to provide a warm, supportive place for people to swap tips and experiences and find love and friendship online."

The NetGirl site offers personal ads, live chat, and regularly scheduled guest interviews.

Flirt's Nook

This is a chat room that is defined, as all chat rooms are, by the quality of its current occupants. Some people have found their soulmates here; others avoid it altogether.

Men Are From Mars, Women From Venus

This site, which you can find by typing Keyword: **Mars**, has as its theme John Gray's book. The site includes a nice little chat room in which people discuss relationships.

Newsgroups

AOL has hundreds of newsgroups targeted to singles in specific cities. Select "Go," then "Keyword," then search for the word "Singles." Find out where all the singles are hiding in your town.

Others

AOL continues to add new features. If you go to the menu bar and select "Go" and then "Keyword" and then type in the word "Keyword," you'll find an extensive list of keywords and descriptions of the corresponding sites.

♥ ♥ ♥

If you select "Go" from the menu bar, then "Keyword," and then type in any keyword that looks interesting to you, you'll go to that site. AOL does not have URL addresses, so it's not always easy to find sites. Using the "Keyword" feature is the easiest way to see many of its features. Also, keep an eye out for new sites that are described on the first screen that pops up after you log on.

The best way to meet people online is to visit those areas that match your interests. Enjoy the conversation and get to know people. "Talk" a lot by email. Many, many people who meet online meet each other in real life. It's a great way to meet people from all over the country in all walks of life...whether you're seeking a love interest or simply want to meet interesting people.

"Doc," an attorney, author, and AOL member, offers this advice: "DO NOT use the areas designated for romance. Rather, it is is far preferable to visit areas in which you have an interest (i.e. movies, music, etc.) and develop relationships with those people At least you can be fairly confident that you will have something in common with the person you meet."

All over the country, people who meet people online hold parties at restaurants and get to know each other in a group (all kinds of people, not neccessarily limited to singles). *It's a great idea!*

♥ ♥ ♥

Keep in mind there are a lot of different people in the world; the first cyber-sweetie you meet most likely won't be the last one you meet. Most people I've spoken to have had several *unsuccessful* relationships before finding Mr. or Ms. Right. The same is true of real life. Finding your soulmate is a journey that cannot be rushed. Enjoy the adventure.

True Stories of Online Romance

Does online romance work? Do people really meet each other and end up in successful, committed relationships? Because the Web is simply an introduction tool, the answer is a resounding, enthusiastic one: *Of course it works!* As in real life, couples meet and fall in love. It's just a matter of finding the right person.

The following stories are true stories of couples who met online. Some of the names have been changed. Ages range from early twenties to mid-fifties.

Rene and Monty
Rene, a high school English/Journalism teacher, met her sweetie, Monty, in a room named for their home state, Minnesota. They began chatting and found they had some acquaintances in common.

Rene writes: "After having a few online romances crash, I was pretty leery of getting involved again. But in this case, I discovered he worked with a friend of mine from high school. It seemed that a few months before we met online...two friends had gotten together and were actually talking about setting Monty and me up. It didn't happen, and I didn't find this out until we had met online. Our relationship online never went beyond the casual chat phase. In fact, we never exchanged phone numbers, last names, or even made plans to meet. We communicated casually for five months. Then we met at a local AOL gathering of people who went in the Minnesota Room."

Monty and Rene found plenty to talk about as they discussed their mutual friends. Rene writes, "The club had a bonfire going outside, and we went there to talk some more. When we came back to the table, everyone else had gone home! We stayed, and talked, and danced, and started a wonderful relationship."

Monty decided to propose to Rene in a unique yet appropriate way. His efforts may still be available at: **http://cp.dullut.mn.us/~monty**, so you can see for yourself! He told her he wanted to show her a cool web site, and he stood behind her as she scrolled down the page to find his proposal.

Rene and Monty's prenuptial celebrations also took on an online twist. Twenty-five of Rene's chat room buddies got together and gave her an "online" wedding shower in one of the AOL chat rooms! I was honored to be invited, and it was a lot of fun! We had decorations: ^**^**^**^** and cups of lime punch: (_)?

The invitations included humorous descriptions of marital situations; the guests were instructed to give Rene "advice" on how to handle these dilemmas, and these creative answers became the guests' presents to Rene. The "shower" conversation was eerily similar to any wedding shower—questions about the wedding plans, and their future, and a lot of good cheer and good wishes.

Teresa and Bob

Teresa and Bob met in the Writers Club area of AOL. I asked Teresa what "attracted" her to Bob online, and she wrote, "I liked the way he described himself physically. ...the fact that we were both interested in writing was important also. And somehow, chemistry with a person comes through when you type!"

Teresa and Bob are now married and have a baby. Her advice to people who may be interested in finding love online: "Take everything with a grain of salt. Think of it as a big party or bar and know that you're most likely going to have hits and misses, just as if you were seeing all of these people face-to-face."

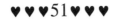

♥ ♥ ♥

Don and Lydia

Don, a writer and computer consultant, and Lydia, a writer, live in Texas. They, too, met in the Writers Club, and chatted online for three months before meeting. Although they enjoyed discussing books and writing, there was no "online attraction."

When Don found out that Lydia, while on vacation, had passed through San Antonio, where he lived, and didn't stop, he extended an invitation via email to meet at a fine Mexican restaurant on the return trip. Don writes: "She walked up behind me when she got there, tapped me on the shoulder. When I turned...I looked into twinkling eyes and was head over heels." Lydia writes: "I KNEW which one he was immediately! We had never been *romantic* online...but there was this...this..electric thing between us immediately."

Don and Lydia now live happily ever after, sitting side by side at their computers, enjoying life together online as well as offline.

Laura and Kris

A year ago, Laura and Kris met each other in the San Diego chat room. The hostess of the room has scheduled a "meeting" of the "roomies" (chat room members) at Foggy's, "a dive bar frequented by Navy squid." Although Laura had seen Kris online in the San Diego room under two different screen names, she never chatted with him until she met him at Foggy's. The evening ended with Kris asking Laura for a date.

Let's pick up the story eight months later: Laura, Kris, and thirteen San Diego chat room members are on a plane enroute to Las Vegas, as part of a fun trip Laura had planned for the group. Kris excuses himself to go the the restroom.

The pilot of the plane announces that there is a special guest on board who wants to make an announcement. Kris, behind a partition, is on the intercom.

♥ ♥ ♥

Laura recalls his words and her reaction: "Kris said, 'In order to provide further entertainment on your trip to Las Vegas, I want to ask a certain special somebody, in seat 2B, a very important question.' He paused dramatically, as I was sliding down into my seat, my cheeks hot. I knew then exactly what he was going to ask. 'Her name is Laura,' he continued, with another pause. 'Laura, will you marry me?' With that, the whole plane gasped." When she said yes, all 120 passengers clapped their approval.

Laura and Kris were married twenty four hours later at a Las Vegas hotel. Present were thirteen of their America Online friends who *thought* they were going to Las Vegas to gamble.

***

All of the couples consider themselves fortunate to have found the love of their lives, and they credit AOL for helping to bring them together. However, they are all quick to point out that online dating should be approached with caution.

♥ ♥ ♥

That First Meeting

So—you've met someone special online and you want to meet face to face? What do you do? First, you read this section. Then, you follow my advice!

If You are in the Same General Region

It's always a good idea to trade photos (exchange .gif files via email) before you decide to meet. If you do decide to meet, make sure you and your cyberfriend are clear on all the details of the meeting: time, address, and duration of the meeting. Meet for coffee in a public place, such as a diner-type restaurant in a mall. If your cyberfriend offers other plans, do not be swayed. Invite a friend to come with you who can lurk nearby. Tell your cyberfriend that your friend is with you, and that you have to leave in an hour or whatever. *Better yet, have a group of his friends meet a group of your friends at a restaurant and have a little after-work party.*

Always keep in mind you are meeting a stranger and you must be careful. Don't let your guard down; otherwise, you may become a victim.

If One Of You is From Out of Town

If You Are Visiting

Always exchange many photos (not just glamorous ones) of each other before you meet.

Tip:
Collect favorite photos of yourself and have them all color copied at your local office supply store on one sheet for about a dollar. That way you don't give up your originals.

Be perfectly honest so there are no unpleasant surprises for either one of you. Most people have some idea of the type of person they are attracted to, and the reality is that for those people, especially men, appearance counts. So be honest.

I'm not saying you have to be a model; not at all! Some men like slender, athletic women. Other men like voluptuous or chubby women. Some feel a woman isn't "sexy" unless she has shoulder-length hair. Or short hair. Or red hair. Or blonde hair and brown eyes. Or nose rings and tattoos.

Some women tell themselves they are not interested in bald or pot-bellied men. Or they love tall, green-eyed blonds. Some women are petite, and they feel strange when they find they are talking to the elbow of a tall man.

My point is that humans are available in an incredible range of colors and sizes, and there is an equally incredible range of preferences...and sometimes, those preconceived "preferences" go by the wayside when you meet someone you just happen to *really* like.

I believe that for everyone, there is someone. So there is no need to disguise who you are or what you look like. Somewhere out there, someone is looking for you.

Do Your Homework

If you know someone in the town you'll be visiting, it's also a good idea to have that person check out your cyber-sweetie—simply verify what your cyber-sweetie has told you.

Have your friend look up his number in the phone book and call it. If a woman answers, you should know if it's his housekeeper or his daughter or whomever. If not, RUN! If your cyberfriend has told you he's a doctor, have your friend look

him up in the phone book to check his office number, or call his affiliated hospital to confirm he is a doctor. Call him at the listed number some time. If it does not compute, RUN! There are liars and con artists (male and female) among the many good people online. You need to take some precautions to avoid being a victim.

One of the first places you may want to check out is **http://www.MostWanted .com** and make sure no one with your cyber-sweetie's description is listed. This is a list of the nation's most-wanted criminals by state. (Yes, I am being sarcastic. But the site is real. Check it out anyway. Hey, you never know.)

You can also use the telephone white pages online, at **http://www.four11.com** and make your own verification calls. If your cyber-sweetie says he owns a business (and if his clients are residential consumers), see if he's listed in the yellow pages: **http://www.imsworld.com/a/yp** or **http://www.bigyellow.com**. If he says he's a professor at a college, find out about the college by checking out **http:www.mit.edu:8001/people/cdemello/univ-full.html**, a list of more than 2,300 college and university home pages.

Just for fun, check out all the search engines at **http://www.search.com** to search his or her name to see if it pops up anywhere. You might also want to see if

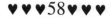

♥ ♥ ♥

it pops up in email data bases: **http://www.iaf.net/** (Internet Address Finder) or **http://sunsite.oit.unc.edu/~masha/** (Finding an Email Address).

If your cyber-sweetie says he (or she) is a doctor or a lawyer or other profession, look up the name online or go to your local library and review the "Who's Who" directories. Ask your librarian for help; librarians know a lot about tracking down information.

Some Very Good Advice to Keep In Mind:

- Do not mess around with **married** people. If your cyber-sweetie still lives with a spouse, don't even think about meeting. In fact, end the relationship. Wait, at least, for the legal separation, and then feel free to invest your time and energy, and to open your heart. But don't hold your breath.

  If you knowingly carry on a romantic relationship with a married person, you will get little sympathy from friends or relatives when your heart is broken, as it most surely will be. Don't do it. You deserve better.

- Keep in mind there are plenty of married people **masquerading as singles**. They are bad news. Once you establish an online relationship, you should be able to call your cyber-sweetie at home or at work at any time. No excuses.

- There are also men masquerading as women, and women as men. Some adults pretend they are children. Many people play this game. Some people carry it to the extreme. Beware.

- If you are **unhappily married**, settle your own life before involving others. Don't become involved with anyone until you end your marriage and are no longer living with your spouse. It's only right. Everyone will be better off for it.

- Keep in mind you are taking a chance on someone if that someone has not allowed at least **two years** to pass to **heal** from the loss of a serious love relationship (such as a marriage). It takes time to get over broken relationships, regardless of how unhappy the relationship was.

- Keep in mind that **you** need time to heal from past relationships. Until you are healed, you are vulnerable. You may make some wrong decisions as you try to replace your old relationship with a new one.

- Always, always, always, *always* be honest. Do not lie about your weight or your height or your age or your profession. Avoid those tangled webs.

♥ ♥ ♥

- *Before deciding to travel long distances to meet each other*, exchange "Welcome to My World" videos. Borrow a camcorder, buy a tape, and have some fun. Start off by taping *yourself* describing what will be in the tape. Pretend your sweetie is at your side, and you're giving a tour. Share images of your home, your pets, your neighborhood, your town, where you work...anything. Keep it light and generic. Make a copy of it before you send it off. Your cyber-sweetie should do the same.

- Before you begin a long-distance relationship, think of what the future may bring. Are you interested in **moving** from your home town—leaving all your friends and relatives? Are you in school and have a couple more years to go until graduation? If you are in school, let me give you this advice: STAY THERE and GRADUATE! If the love is real, it will survive the test of time.

  Think, too, about how you will maintain a long-distance relationship. Do you have **extra money** for long distance phone bills? Airfare? Time off from work or school to make trips? Don't set yourself up for heartache. Think this through. You may wish to make friends with people from across the country, and enjoy those cyber-friendships. You may reserve your romantic interests, however, to people closer to home. (Cold, you say? No. Life is a succession of decisions; you need to make realistic decisions to avoid a lifetime of heartache.)

♥ ♥ ♥

- Before your romantic relationship truly blossoms (and before you've invested time and telephone/airline money) ask your potential cyber-sweetie **for names and phone numbers** of three people in his (or her) life, such as siblings, parents, friends or co-workers. Say you simply want to talk to *them* so you can better know *him* (or *her*). Call and ask questions to confirm what your sweetie told you. Provide the same information if asked.

- No matter what your cyber-sweetie's story is, **NEVER loan, or give away, any money**. Never. If your cyber-sweetie can't afford to visit you, suggest a part-time job and a savings account. Greyhound often has good deals (**http:// www. greyhound.com/index.html**). Perhaps there is some money sitting around in a forgotten bank account in your cyber-sweetie's name. Find out at **http://www.foundmoney.com.**

cathy®

by **Cathy Guisewite**

♥ ♥ ♥

If You Are Hosting

It's a good idea to limit a visit to a weekend. Plan a fun-filled Saturday, and keep Sunday open. Your visitor may want to go home early. *You* may want your visitor to go home early.

No matter how tempting, do not:

- invite your cyber-sweetie to stay at your home
- accept an offer to share a hotel room.

You will never regret it!

Instead of seeing this meeting as a romantic rendezvous, consider it an opportunity to get to know each other better and an opportunity to either discover a new city or share your hometown. Make sure you make this 100% clear to your cyberfriend. If it is not acceptable, by all means, revoke the invitation!

When you're alone and lonely, you are extremely vulnerable. Recognize your vulnerability and protect yourself, emotionally and physically.

If you have children, get a relative or friend to take them for the day. Do not involve your family with your new friend. Not yet.

♥ ♥ ♥

I have heard too many stories (from women) who have opened their hearts to men they met online. The men take full advantage of the women's hospitality: they stay at their homes, eat their food, tour their city, meet the family, and enjoy their company. Some of these visits lasts for days. Everything seems rosy and romantic and loving and just peachy keen. Then the man returns to his home and apparently falls off the face of the earth, never to be heard from again. The woman is devastated.

Why does this happen? Well, the man may be married. More likely, the relationship developed too quickly. The man returned home and decided that he did not want to continue the relationship; he found it easier to ignore the woman than to face the painful chore of explaining his decision. He may have truly enjoyed the time spent with her, but when he re-enters his "real life," he realizes that continuing the relationship is not feasible. So take my advice. Go slowly.

Wait! Before we talk any more about visits, I want you to read the next section, "Is it Love?"

Is It Love?

The Web and commercial online services have made a dramatic effect on the dynamics of our society, especially the way we communicate with each other.

The advantage to online romance is that men and women often fall in love with each others' brains, and not their bodies. They get to know each others' personalities before there is any physical attraction.

Many people who meet online experience an intense attraction and connection to one another. They often feel that the person they met is absolutely perfect for them. They believe they have finally stumbled upon their soulmates.

In a short time online, a couple can get to know each other at a very intimate level. They share their thoughts, hopes, dreams, needs, wants and desires.

Compare this cyber-relationship to a typical "real-life" relationship. You may meet at work. Exchange shy glances for weeks. Ask co-workers about each others' personal situations. One finally gets up the courage to ask the other out for lunch or coffee. You go out, have fun, and slowly you get to know each other. You talk on the phone. You may become physically intimate; but it may be months before you get to exploring the deeper level of your emotions. Online, it can take days, or even hours.

Online, there is nothing between you and the other person's emotions. You don't have to worry about dressing up, going out, worrying about what the other thinks about how you look. No sweaty palms, no body odor, no bad breath. No nervousness, because you're just sitting in front of your computer at home. You have no other activity except to explore each other's thoughts.

The result is often a feeling of deep connection with the other person. Is it love? It feels like love. It seems unbelievable to you that you DO feel like you're in love—with someone you never met! You may never have even seen a photo of the person! What's going on?

STOP, and before you go any further, commit these words to memory:

> *Until you meet in real life, it's nothing but cyberfatuation.*

♥ ♥ ♥

Are you really in love? The answer is NO! You are experiencing a very normal reaction, and it could very well end up being the beginnings of love. I call it **cyberfatuation**, not love, and it is not (yet) a healthy base for a lasting love. Cyberfatuation is unique state of emotion: it is infatuation as the result of a cyberfantasy.

You've no doubt heard this before: "The most powerful human sex organ is the one found between the ears." No statement could be truer when applied to online romance.

When you meet someone online, you have just a few clues: a screen name, a writing (and typing) style, a few well-chosen words in the profile. You may even have downloaded a photo of your cyber-sweetie. You have an extremely limited view of this person. So your brain fills in all the details.

Your imagination is very powerful. With just a few cues, you create an image of this person in your mind. You then believe this person will fulfill the expectations you've created. (*Oh, he's so sweet and sensitive and romantic and loving and witty and giving*.) He may very well be Mr. Perfect. More likely, you simply do not know him well enough to make a better-informed assessment.

♥ ♥ ♥

This persona you have created, and these expectations that you have unwittingly identified, may exist and survive throughout the engagement period, straight through the honeymoon, and well into the first several months of the marriage. Your cyber-sweetie may—or may not—meet all your expectations. The trouble starts when the expectations are not met.

He loves your relatives...except for your mother. He loves dogs, but has no use for Yvonne, your yappy little Yorkie. You pay the bills, and he gives you some money for his share, but you're not quite sure how much money he actually brings home. He loves you dearly, or so he says, but he sometimes disappears and doesn't tell you where he's gone. Or he uses the computer for hours at a time, and he won't tell you exactly what he's doing, but you know in your heart the truth. You don't know how much you can take. He's nothing like you expected. *WHAT HAPPENED?*

This is what happened: You were cyberfatuated. You were in a heightened state of unawareness and your brain was mush. You decided to marry when you were in this state (also often mistaken for being "in love.")

You simply cannot make such a big important decision as getting married when your brain is mush.

♥ ♥ ♥

So what does one do to avoid this potential for disaster? The answer is: **Take it slowly.** Get to know each other. Ask and discuss all the questions in this book. Base your decisions on reality, not your assumptions.

Be especially slow, too, about physical intimacy. It may all seem so romantic, but nothing is romantic about sexually transmitted diseases. *There is also nothing more heartbreaking than to be physically intimate with someone and then never to hear from that person again.* Force yourself to think about life's harsh realities when you least want to think about them. **You will never regret doing so.**

Okay, I got <u>that</u> out of my system. So now, back to The Visit...

What You <u>Should</u> Do During the Visit

Most cities have a section in the front of their phone books with all kinds of information about fun things to do, many of which you have probably never experienced. Now's the time! Plan a picnic to a local park; go swimming at the closest beach. Show off your biggest mall. Drive around your fanciest neighborhood. If a festival is in town, go to it.

If you're from a big city, go to the most well-known or tackiest tourist haunts. Plan the whole day with fun things to do. Top it off with your favorite meal at your favorite restaurant.

Tip:
Plan a Saturday night event (meet at a restaurant or club) with **your friends** and your cyber-sweetie. Your friends will ask nosy questions, and you can see how your sweetie reacts to others.

♥ ♥ ♥

Keep everything low key and casual. You may want to visit **http://www.dinesite.com** to see if any of the restaurants in your town are listed.

Avoid going to a movie, unless it's one that has had great reviews that you both want to see. Otherwise, you miss two hours to get to know each other. However, if you feel you need a two-hour break from talking to each other, by all means, go to a movie. (Two days is a long first date.) For information on movies, take a look at **http://www.film.com** or **http://lyre/mit.edu/~deering/tpark.html.**

Find out if there will be a special concert or other live event in town that you may both be interested in by checking out **http://www.ticketmaster.com**.

In general, just HAVE FUN. The visit is for you get to know each other in real life. You already know each other on one level. Now you can see how each other looks, sounds, moves, smells, acts, and reacts. Don't worry about the future. Just enjoy the weekend. You need time to "digest" all the information you acquire over the weekend before you can make logical decisions for the future. Just enjoy the moment.

If the relationship works out, congratulations! If it doesn't, don't blame yourself. If your cyber-sweetie decides to end the relationship, recognize that he or she was simply not the right person for you. The right person IS out there for you.

If you are the one ending the relationship, be extremely sensitive to your friend's feelings. Whether you break the news in person or by phone, do it with great care and tenderness. (Don't do it by email!)

Another tip: Do not fall off the face of the earth; the minimum you owe that person is a sense of closure. You don't have to go into fine detail as to why you don't want to continue the relationship; but it's better to take responsibility for your decision, instead of focusing on *your perceptions* of the other person's shortcomings. "I just don't think we're a good match" is an acceptable phrase.

Keeping Love Alive When You're Far Apart

When you do find a cyber-sweetie, and you're further than a tank of gas away, it becomes a challenge to maintain the relationship. The couples I've talked to who met online spent a large amount of cash on email time as well as telephone time. To save money, you may wish to:

- Use an Internet service provider with one monthly charge for unlimited email service and Web access.

- Find a small company that buys telephone time and resells it at cheaper rates. (It's a confusing concept, but it's real.) There may be some restrictions, but if you qualify, it's worth signing up, since those pennies-per-hour charges quickly add up. Call up your local Chamber of Commerce and ask if there are any "long distance resellers" on their member list. Always compare their rates with the major phone companies; sometimes the big companies have special deals the resellers can't beat.

- Try out the free phone services available on the Web that bypass the phone company, such as **http://www.freetel.com**. (Well worth the effort!)

In between telephone and email time, you may want to try the following:

1. Send an occasional handwritten note on good stationery. Email is nice, but handwritten letters are *much* nicer.
2. Send greeting cards or make your own cards.
3. Send a Web postcard. You'll find them at **http://postcards.www.media.mit.edu/Postcards/** or check out **http://www.online-romance.com** for other ideas. Or make your own online card at **http://www.buildacard.com.**
4. Send virtual flowers: **http://www.virtualflowers.com**
5. Watch the same TV shows and discuss them later.
6. Discuss current events after browsing the newspapers at **http://www.enews.com/** or go directly to USA Today at **http://www.usatoday.com**

7. Play games listed at **http://www.whiterock.com/kinglink/.** (King Link and Games)
8. On a Friday or Saturday night, rent the same movie. Afterwards, enjoy a cup of decaf as you discuss the movie online. For movie ideas, go to **http://www.film.com/**
9. Send home-baked cookies or brownies.
10. Send real flowers: **http://www. flowers.com**
11. Email a love letter with a little help: **http://home. havisoft.com/loeandromance/page13.htm** or **http:www.nando.net/toys/cyrano.html**. Make sure you tell your cyber-sweetie that the words may not be yours, but the feelings are.
12. Create a web site together; search the Internet for royalty-free graphics and ideas. (All AOL members can have their own web sites.)
13. Together, answer the questions listed in this book.
14. Go to **http://www.search.com** and search for "real estate" and pretend you're buying a luxury home. Compare choices.
15. Visit an art museum on the web and later compare favorite paintings. See **http://ww.crl.com/~philip/Arthome.html.**
16. Direct your sweetie to your favorite love poem: **http:www.ece.ucdavis.edu/~darsie/ library/.html** or **http:www.hooked.net/users/sven/poets.corner.html**
17. Send video letters to each other.

♥ ♥ ♥

More Online Romance
Words of Wisdom

1. Think of online romance as an **introduction tool**, nothing more. It is not magic. It is simply an easy way to meet and get to know a lot of different people.

2. **Never lie.** You'll pay for it later.

3. **Do not believe everything** you hear, such as gender, age, marital status, weight, occupation, and location. Remember there are male and female con artists and criminals everywhere, even online. People *have* been victims of crime after meeting an online person in real life.

   Although *most* people online are good people, just like in real life, there are bad people. You just have to take precautions.

4. Consider any online relationship, at first, as an online **friendship**. (You can still call each other cyber-sweeties.) Consider it a romantic relationship ONLY after you have met and decided to continue the relationship. If it doesn't work out romantically, you still have a friend.

♥ ♥ ♥

5. **NEVER** give out your address or phone number until you have followed all the advice in this book, and your cyberfriend has earned your trust. (That may take months.) A post office box number and an unlisted phone number are good ideas.

6. Don't wait too long before you talk on the phone. You'll learn a lot from each other's voices.

7. Do not have a "hot" anonymous online relationship with someone. Could be your boss. Or a neighbor, or your cousin Pat. Or you could be talking to an eleven-year-old kid. It's important to find out exactly with whom you are dealing.

8. If you have high standards for finding someone physically attractive, spend a day at the mall on a Saturday. Watch the incredible variety of humanity walk by. Occasionally you may find someone you think is beautiful. You must remember that the people online are normal people, just like the ones you see at the mall or at work or next to you at the stoplight. Movies stars and models are movie stars and models because they are usually *exceptionally* beautiful.

   On the other hand, do not think for a moment that people online are people who can't find a date in real life. The people I've met online are, in real life, professional, articulate, intelligent, and attractive.

♥ ♥ ♥

9. Before spending money on traveling to meet each other, exchange casual (not just "glamour") photos and videos. When you meet for the first time, you should already know what the other looks like through the photos and videos. This a time to get to know each other, not a time for surprises.

10. Keep in mind that appearance *does* count; the goal is to find someone who likes your appearance, regardless of what you look like. If you lie about your weight or your age, even a little, you are simply postponing rejection and multiplying your pain.

11. When you meet the first time, the best option is to meet in a group, such as a party or get-together at a restaurant. If not in a group, then bring a friend along to wait for you. Schedule the first meeting for no longer than an hour. **Always meet in a public place.**

12. Remember that until you meet (and quite often even after that), you are **not** in love. You are cyberfatuated. **Cyberfatuation** is temporary. **Reserve decisions on all major life choices**, such as moving and marrying.

13. Beware of married people pretending to be single. They play with fire. They know not the damage they cause to everyone around them. They have no respect for their spouses, the people they meet online, or themselves.

♥ ♥ ♥

If you know someone is married and you carry on a "harmless" online affair with that person, you, too, are a fool. The computer is not a magazine or a book. There are real people behind those words, and **real hearts that ache when broken**.

14. People usually need at least **two** years to heal from the loss of love (as in a marriage). You need to wait for that time to pass. Otherwise, you are simply a rebound fling and will most likely be eventually tossed aside. Protect yourself and avoid such situations. You can do better.

15. Never end an online relationship by dropping out of sight. Do not close your Internet account or change your email address as a way to avoid talking to someone you don't want to "cyber-date" anymore. **This is cruel.** Anyone who was kind enough to be interested in you deserves a sense of closure—a sensitive "goodbye" at least. Don't blame the other person. It is not that person's fault if he or she does not fulfill *your* requirements.

16. Always keep in mind one of my favorite phrases: ***For everyone, there is someone.***

17. Get a fast modem.

Romance Web Sites

If you find that some of the web sites listed in this book don't work, it's probably because the Web is dependent on millions of individuals for its upkeep and maintenance and is always "under construction."

If you search for "Personals" on the web (using the Alta Vista search engine found on www.search.com), you'll find hundreds of listings. Among them, you'll find sleazy 900 services offering phone sex and offers to fix you up with beautiful Asian or Russian women (it'll only cost you a few thousand dollars and a trip to the other side of the world). It's overwhelming and can be quite depressing. Don't give up. You *will* find good people online. You just have to know where to look.

> **Tip:**
> If any Web address doesn't work for you, **enter the title of the site** (example: "Maczynski's Info Source") in a search engine, such as Alta Vista, to search for it. Often this works when you can't get through using the address.

♥ ♥ ♥

Some Fun Romance-related Sites

Online-Romance Central
http://www.online-romance.com
The absolute best online romance site in the entire world!!!! Okay, I admit it...this is MY web site. Take a look at my Electronic Antique Postcards™ and send one to your cyber-sweetie! (Most of the cards are from about 1910; they're hysterical.) I hope to build this site into one of the most-fun sites on the Internet. Take a look and let me know what you think...I'm listening!

The World of Romance and Greg Godek
http://www.godek.com
Author and King of Romance Greg Godek is one of my favorite personalities. His website offers romance links and excerpts from his books on romance and how to be romantic. A lot of fun!

Love Life Radio Network (in Hawaii)
http://www.lovelife.com
Chat room, romance links. A little bit of Hawaii on the net.

Princess Diane page with Romance links
http://www.iguide.com/internet/features/dater.htm
 Wouldn't we all like to fix her up with a nice guy?

♥ ♥ ♥

Some Matchmaking Sites:

Match.com
http://www.match.com
Personal ads, relationship zine, boutique. Free trial membership, reasonable rates.

Cupid's Network
http://www.cupidnet.com/cupid.
Personal ads, romance info.

Web Match
http://www.webmatch.com

The WebPersonals
http://www.webpersonals.com

The Internet Personals
http://www.motagar.com/personals/index.html

Tip:
If at all possible, try to limit your search to those people who live in your neck of the woods. As far as the "Asian (or Russian) Ladies Available" web sites, it's a bit difficult (time consuming, risky, and very expensive) to arrange a first-time "get-to-know-you" cup of coffee meeting with people who live on the other side of the world. Better to meet someone stateside and use any available cash for an incredible honeymoon!

♥ ♥ ♥

Other Very Useful Sites:

Arlene H. Rinaldi
"I'm NOT Miss Manners of the Internet" (or so she claims)
Everything you need to know about etiquette on the net. Read this before you surf anywhere!
http://rs6000.adm.fau.edu/rinaldi/netiquette.html

Tile.net
http://www.tile.net/
A great list of links to mailing lists, Usenet newsgroups, and FTP sites.

Electronic Library
http:www.elibrary.com
Subscription cost, but searches newspapers, magazines and other sources for any information you want.

Maczynski's Info Source (LOTS of links!!!)
http://www.basenet/net/~tci/pages.html

cathy®

Getting-To-Know-You Questions For Your Cyber-Sweetie!

The questions in this section are a lot of fun as well as very important. You can select questions to get to know your sweetie on many levels.

I recommend that you:

1. Answer the questions *yourself* on a separate piece of paper. (You may be surprised at your answers!)
2. Mark the subject areas that are *most important to you* in a relationship.
3. When you're getting to know someone, **first ask those questions that are most important to *you***.
4. Before you spend big bucks (e.g. airfare, hotel) to meet in real life, go through the *entire* book. Match your cyber-sweetie's answers with yours.
5. Take a long hard look at what life will be like with a person who thinks like your cyber-sweetie. Keep in mind your cyber-sweetie will not change. Trust me.

How to Ask the Questions While Online

You can either type out the questions to your cyber-sweetie—or—you can send your cyber-sweetie his or her own copy of the book. (Or better yet, have your cyber-sweetie order it.) Call 1-800-828-6772 for fastest service. Other ways to order the book are in the back of this book.

If you each have a copy of the book, you then need only to type in the **number** of the question, and then you and your sweetie can take turns answering. Saves a lot of typing (and online time) for a measly U.S.$6.95 (plus shipping, handling, and applicable taxes). :)

It's important that you ask your cyber-sweetie all these questions if you are considering a committed relationship. After all, you want to *avoid* having to go to **http://www.divorce-online.com.**

There are a lot of questions here, from silly to serious. The silly ones are a lot of fun, and the serious ones give you an opportunity to ask questions you might never have otherwise asked, but you *need* to ask.

♥ ♥ ♥

What do you do if you think your cyber-sweetie is lying to you? You should express that sentiment to your sweetie via e-mail. If you still think he or she is lying, I think you should write a "Dear John (or Jane)" email, cancel your online account, and tuck your keyboard under your arm and cyber-run the other way! If you don't trust the person now, it will only get worse.

Trust your instincts. If something doesn't seem quite right, you know it probably isn't. Also, keep in mind the following three little words of wisdom that Oprah Winfrey has shared on her show:

> **Love doesn't hurt.**

If someone is lying to you, ridiculing you, hitting you, cheating on you, or in any way emotionally or physically abusing you, *that person does not deserve your love and attention.* That person may *say* he or she loves you, but it is not true love, and **you deserve true love**.

Now, on to the questions!

♥ ♥ ♥

First Things First

1. Do you agree to truthfully answer the questions in this book?

Marital History

2. Are you single (never married)?

3. Are you separated? Do you have a legal separation? How long have you been separated?

4. Are you legally divorced?

5. Are you legally married?

6. Are you still living with your spouse?

7. If you are married and living with your spouse, why are you wasting my time answering these questions?

   If you have been married and are now divorced...

8. How many times have you been married?

♥ ♥ ♥

9. Are you a somewhat changed person as a result of your previous marriage(s)?

10. Why do you think your previous marriage(s) ended?

11. Would you do some things differently if you were to remarry? *(Please explain.)*

Work

12. Do you work? What do you do?

13. What is a typical day for you?

14. What do you like best about it? Least?

15. Do you like your manager and co-workers?

16. How did you happen to get into that line of work?

17. What would you change about your job if you could change it?

18. How long have had this job? Do you have any plans to change?

19. Do you have any other career interests?

Leisure Activities

20. Do have very much time for leisure activities?

21. Do you enjoy concerts? If so, what kind of music?

22. Do you like to go out to dinner?

23. Do you mind spending money on hobbies you enjoy?

24. What are your hobbies?

25. What hobbies would you like to pursue if you had the time and money?

26. Do you enjoy your work so much that you prefer to work when you have any free time?

27. Do you like playing around on your computer? Do you spend a lot of time on your computer? How much time a day?

28. Do you enjoy watching movies at movie theaters?

29. Do you avoid going out to the movies because it's so much cheaper to rent videos?

30. Do you like to be punctual; are you usually early to an event or social gathering?

31. Do you think that people who are often late to events or social gatherings are rude?

32. Do you watch TV sports every week?

33. Do you enjoy attending sports events?

34. Do you enjoy participating in athletic events?

35. Do you expect your partner to participate in athletic events with you?

36. Do you like to listen to music? What type? How loud? What format? Radio? Tape? CD?

37. Do you like clothes shopping?

38. Do you expect your partner to go clothes shopping with you?

39. Do you enjoy visiting "bed and breakfast" inns?

40. Do you like doing "touristy" things when you travel?

41. Do you prefer to stay in a hotel, rather than go camping, during your vacations?

42. Do you like to get as far away from people as you possibly can when you go on vacation?

43. Describe your ideal vacation.

44. Do you like gambling?

45. Do you set aside money to gamble every week?

46. Do you may spend a lot of money gambling, but you win most of it back?

47. Do you like RV (recreational vehicle) camping?

48. Do you enjoy fishing and boating?

49. Do you enjoy gardening?

50. Do you enjoy going to museums?

51. Do you expect your partner to share all your interests?

52. During vacations, do you enjoy staying home?

53. Do you enjoy traveling?

54. Would you rather stay home in peace and quiet than go to a crowded public event?

55. Do you like to watch television? How many hours a day? What are your favorite shows? Explain why you like them.

56. Do you believe it is healthy and acceptable if you and your partner each wish to pursue your own separate interests?

57. Are you interested in stock car races, rodeos, air shows, or tractor pulls?

58. Do you enjoy plays, movies, art shows, or community events?

59. Are you interested in white water rafting, parachuting, skiing, horseback riding, or rock climbing?

60. Do you like football, basketball, baseball or soccer? Why or why not?

61. Do you enjoy sampling a little bit of all types of events?

Holidays

62. Do you enjoy celebrating holidays?

63. What are your favorite holidays? Why?

64. Do you enjoy celebrating anniversaries?

65. Do you celebrate the holidays of your religion?

66. If you do not celebrate the holidays of your religion, do you hope to do so some day?

67. Would you be very unhappy if your partner forgot your birthday or an anniversary?

68. Do you believe it is important to put aside money throughout the year in order to purchase high-quality gifts during the winter holidays?

69. Do you think people spend too much money on holiday gifts?

70. Do you enjoy giving people expensive gifts?

71. Do you enjoy giving people gifts, not necessarily expensive gifts?

♥ ♥ ♥

72. Would you be very sad if your partner did not remember you with flowers, candy, or at least a card on St. Valentine's Day?

73. Do you spend major holidays with your parent(s)? Would you consider other options?

74. Would you be unhappy if your partner gave you a low-cost holiday present?

75. Do you think the cost of a present is not important and the thought behind it is what is important?

76. Would you be unhappy if your partner gave you a present that did not match any of your needs or preferences, indicating he or she did not put much thought into selecting it?

77. Do you think that gifts of kindness and loving deeds have more value than material gifts? Or do you think that's just an excuse for cheapness?

78. Do you think the holidays are a great time to buy a nice gift for your partner to express appreciation for the gifts of kindness and loving deeds he or she gave you throughout the year?

♥ ♥ ♥

Cars

79. What kind of car do you drive?

80. Is it important that you drive a nice, relatively new car?

81. Do you think it's important to buy the best car you can possibly afford?

82. Would you be embarrassed to be seen riding in or driving an old rusty car?

83. Do you prefer buying new cars or used cars?

84. What is your ideal car?

85. Do you like to fix cars?

86. Do you think the make and model of a car are not as important as the car's dependability?

87. Do you always buckle your seat belt?

88. It is important to keep the interior and exterior of your vehicle clean at all times?

89. Do you like pickup trucks?

90. Do you like motorcycles?

Pets

91. In general, do you like most pets?

92. Do you like dogs as pets?

93. Do you like cats as pets?

94. It would bother you to see a cat sleeping on a kitchen or dining room table?

95. Does it bother you when dogs jump up on you when you visit friends' homes?

96. Does it bother you when you see someone place a dinner dish on the floor so a dog or cat can finish the scraps?

97. Are you (or children in your family) allergic to cats and/or other animals?

98. Do you think the homes of people who have *cats* have a distinct and unpleasant odor?

♥ ♥ ♥

99. Do you think the homes of people who have *dogs* have a distinct and unpleasant odor?

100. Would you ever own a dog that regularly drooled?

101. Do you enjoy sleeping with your pet(s)?

102. What is your ideal pet?

103. Would you ever consider having three or more dogs at one time?

104. Do you like exotic pets?

105. Do you like birds or fish as pets?

106. Would it bother you to have a partner who enjoyed fish or birds?

107. Would you prefer not to have any pets?

Romance

108. Do you think daily hugging and kissing are extremely important in a relationship?

109. Would you feel hurt if your partner did not say "I love you" at least once a day?

110. What does it mean to you when someone says "I love you" ?

111. Do you think that if a man says he "wants some romance," he usually wants sex?

112. Do you think that if a woman says she "wants some romance," she usually wants loving attention and tenderness?

113. Do you think that flowers, candlelight dinners, and sweet little surprises are a vital part of keeping romance alive in a relationship? Or do you think they are scenarios thought up by major greeting card companies?

114. Do you like receiving flowers?

115. Are you allergic to flowers? Are you allergic to anything?

116. Do you think that if you treat your partner with respect at all times, there is no need for any stereotypical "romantic" episodes?

117. What do you think is romantic?

118. Do you think long, slow kisses are romantic?

119. Do you think it is romantic for a couple to have the same bedtime (one person should not stay up later than the other, if possible)?

120. Name five things you think are romantic.

121. Name five things you think are sexy.

122. Do you enjoy receiving back massages?

123. Do you enjoy giving back massages?

124. Do you believe it is important for a man and woman to give each other massages, because a massage is a loving and romantic gesture?

125. Should displays of affection (kissing, holding hands) be done only while in the home and not in public?

126. After a couple is married, do you think it is necessary to do the romantic things they did before they were married?

127. Do you agree with the statement, "Love conquers all"?

128. Do you think that there is just one "perfect person" in the world for each person? Or do you think that we have the capability to love many types of people?

♥ ♥ ♥

Personal Etiquette

129. Do you think it's rude to pass gas in front of other people, especially one's partner?

130. Are you an unusually gaseous person?

131. Do you love to make jokes about passing gas?

132. Do you have tattoos? Body piercing? If so, where? If not, do you have any plans for such enhancements?

133. Do you spit in public?

134. Do you flick cigarette butts out your car window at stop lights (or any time)?

135. Do you think it is rude to burp in front of others, including one's partner?

136. Do you think that all burps should be accompanied with an "Excuse me" by the burper to the burpee?

137. Do you use toothpicks in public?

138. Do you use dental floss in public?

139. Do you have any habits that drive other people nuts?

140. If your partner had bad breath, would you tell your partner or would you simply end the relationship and leave your partner wondering for all eternity what went wrong?

141. Do you adjust your underwear in public when you think no one is looking?

142. Do you think a man should shave daily?

143. If you are female, do you prefer kissing a clean-shaven face or a bearded face?

144. Should women maintain clean-shaven underarms and legs?

145. If you are male, how important is it that your partner's arms and legs are clean shaven?

146. Do you keep your ears and nose free of sprouting hairs?

147. Do you hate it when women wear too much make up?

148. Do you hate it when women don't wear enough make up?

♥ ♥ ♥

149. Do you think body odor is normal and natural and should not be disguised with perfumes and deodorants?

150. Do you think daily showers or baths are a necessity for both men and women?

151. Do you ever sneeze into a cloth napkin at a dinner table? Do you know that's really gross?

152. If anyone sneezes near you, do you feel compelled to say, "God bless you"?

153. If you sneeze and someone fails to say "God bless you!" does it ruin your entire day?

154. Do you believe a man and woman should display proper table manners when dining with each other, even when there is no one else around? Or is it okay to pick up your soup and slurp? Or slide corn on the cob on top of a stick of butter?

155. Do you take everything seriously?

156. Do you like to laugh?

♥ ♥ ♥

157. What makes you laugh?

Basic Beliefs

158. Do you believe in God?

159. Do you go to church every week?

160. Is religion important to you?

161. Would you prefer to marry someone of your faith?

162. Would you expect your intended to convert to your religion?

163. Do you have friends who are atheist or agnostic?

164. If you are religious, do you ever try to convert other people?

165. Do you say prayers at mealtimes at home? In restaurants?

166. Do you pity people who believe in a religion other than your own?

167. Do you believe your religion is the only true religion?

168. Do you believe it is your responsibility to share the word of God?

♥ ♥ ♥

169. **Do you think that no one religion is necessarily right or wrong and everyone is entitled to an opinion?**

170. **Do you mind it if people try to convert you to their religion?**

171. **Do you enjoy watching religious programs on TV?**

172. **If you had children, would you want to bring them up in your religion?**

173. **Do you enjoy discussing philosophical ideas?**

174. **Do you consider yourself a spiritual person?** (If yes, explain.)

175. **Do you believe in the supernatural?**

176. **Do you think most people cheat on their taxes?**

177. **Do you believe it is nobody's business (including the government's) how much money you make?**

178. **Is it okay to steal small items, such as pens, tape dispensers, and staplers, from your employer?**

179. **Do you think it is extremely important that a husband and wife never lie to each other?**

180. Is it okay to lie once in a while if it doesn't hurt anyone?

181. Is it normal for people to have extramarital affairs?

182. Do you realize that if you were married and cheated on your spouse, you risk losing your spouse, your way of life, as well as a lot of money? (Note: You may wish to define with your partner your exact definition of "cheating.")

183. If you were married, how would you feel if your spouse had "cybersex" with others? Is that considered cheating?

Politics

184. If you had to choose one political party that most closely matches your beliefs, which one would it be?

185. Do you always vote along party lines?

186. Do you consider yourself a liberal?

187. Do you consider yourself conservative?

188. Do you consider yourself a moderate?

♥ ♥ ♥

189. Do you believe it is important for your partner to share your political views?

190. Do you would like someday to become more knowledgeable about politics?

191. Would you like someday to become more involved in politics?

192. Do you think all politicians are crooks?

Guns

193. Do you own a gun?

194. Do you think it's important that all citizens be armed?

195. Do you think the main reason violence is a problem in our society is because too many people have guns?

196. Do you think gun control laws should be stricter?

197. Should toy guns should be banned? Would you buy one for your child?

198. Do you enjoy hunting?

♥ ♥ ♥

Education and The World Around Us

199. Do you avoid reading the newspaper because you believe it contains nothing but bad news?

200. Do you try to read the newspaper every day?

201. Do you enjoy watching local and national TV news?

202. Do you listen to the radio to hear about local and world events?

203. Do you often read books?

204. Do you often read magazines?

205. Do you hate to read?

206. Do you believe that continuing education (gaining knowledge about the world), for people of any age, is important?

207. Do you believe a college education is very important?

208. Are you uncomfortable around people who are not educated?

209. Do you believe an advanced degree is very important?

210. Do you think some educated people are snobs?

211. If you had children, would you insist that they complete a college education?

Race

212. What are your thoughts about living in a racially mixed neighborhood?

213. Would you have any objection to your (adult) child marrying a person of a race different from your own?

214. Would you have any objection if your child wanted to date a person of a race different from your own?

215. Do you believe the races should be separate?

216. Have you ever been a victim of racism or sexism?

217. If you were an apartment owner, would you rent an apartment to a person of a race different from your own?

218. Do you believe there is anything wrong with interracial marriage?

219. Do you trust people outside your race?

220. Do you believe all people are equal and should be treated the same?

221. Do you believe character, not the color of a person's skin, is what matters?

222. Do you have friends of a race different from your own?

223. If given the opportunity, would you have any objection to *hiring* someone of a race different from your own?

224. Would you have any objection to *working* for someone of a race different from your own?

225. Why do you think some people are racist?

Acceptance of Gay People

226. Are you angered by people who are intolerant of gay and lesbian people?

227. Are you uncomfortable around gay or lesbian people?

228. Do you believe homosexuality is a lifestyle choice?

229. Would you hire a gay or lesbian person?

230. Do you believe that people who hate gay and/or lesbian people do so out of ignorance and irrational fear?

♥ ♥ ♥

231. If you believe the sexual behavior of gay and lesbian people is unacceptable, is it because of your religious convictions?

232. If you found out that a friend of yours was gay, would you continue the friendship? What about a brother or a sister?

233. If your partner had a gay or lesbian friend or relative, would you avoid that person?

234. If your adult child told you he or she was gay/lesbian, what would you do? Would your child still be welcome in your home?

235. Should people be judged on character and not on sexual orientation?

Friends

236. Should a husband and wife be each other's best friend?

237. Is it healthy if a person has many different types of people in his or life?

238. In a good marriage, does either partner need anyone else but each other?

239. Have you ever been jealous of the time your partner spends with his or her friends?

♥ ♥ ♥ 111 ♥ ♥ ♥

♥ ♥ ♥

240. When two people marry, should they go out with their single friends as they did before they married?

241. Is it possible for a person to have a member of the opposite sex as a very good friend and not be lovers?

242. Once someone is married, should that person stop daily contact with his or her parents?

243. If you are in a romantic relationship, would you stop going out with your friends on a regular basis?

244. If you didn't like you partner's friends, would you simply ignore them?

245. Do you like to joke about your partner's shortcomings?

246. Do you think it's important never to insult your partner (even jokingly), especially in front of other people?

247. Do you think it may not be a good idea to discuss your relationship problems with your friends and relatives? Do you think they would be able to forgive your partner as easily as you would?

♥ ♥ ♥

248. When you get angry, do you like to express your feelings or do you prefer to be alone?

Food

249. Do you expect your partner to be a good cook?

250. Do you like to cook?

251. Do you enjoy eating at home?

252. Are you a vegetarian? If so, do you mind fixing meals with meat for your partner?

253. If you are a vegetarian, what are your reasons for becoming one?

254. Describe table manners that drive you crazy.

255. Do you prefer a "meat and potato" type of a meal over anything else?

256. Do you enjoy eating at restaurants?

257. Are you fussy about what you eat?

258. Do you like trying ethnic foods (such as Chinese, Vietnamese, Korean, Greek, Indian, Mexican)?

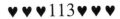

Clothing

259. Do you enjoy wearing the latest fashions?

260. Do you expect your partner to dress in up-to-date styles?

261. Would you be embarrassed to be seen in public with your partner if your partner wore old, dirty, or ripped clothes?

262. Do you believe women should always dress in a sexy way?

263. Do you believe women should always dress in a conservative way?

264. Should a woman should dress to please her man?

265. Do you believe there are some situations in which it is acceptable for a man or a woman to dress in a sexy way? What is sexy to you?

266. Should a man dress to please his woman?

267. Should people dress to please themselves?

268. Are you shy about nudity?

269. Do you often walk around nude at home?

270. Would it bother you to have your partner walk around nude at home?

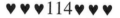

♥ ♥ ♥

271. Would you enjoy visiting a beach where clothing was optional?

272. Do you believe there should be laws to prevent women from walking around topless in public?

273. Do you find it disturbing when you see mothers nurse their infants in public?

274. Are you uncomfortable when you see nude art displayed in someone's home?

Shelter

275. Do you prefer living in an apartment rather than a house?

276. It is important to you to own your home?

277. Do you now own your home?

278. Do you enjoy doing basic plumbing or electrical work?

279. Do you enjoy gardening?

280. Would you like to live in a contemporary-style home?

281. Would like to live in a rustic-style home?

♥ ♥ ♥

282. Do you like decorating your home with flea market and garage sale items?

283. Is it important to you to have nice (new) furniture, rugs, and wallpaper?

284. Do you prefer living in the country?

285. Do you prefer living in the city?

286. Do you prefer living in a suburban area?

287. Do you prefer antiques and old furniture with character?

288. Do you prefer purchasing new furniture and decorative accessories?

289. Do you like to spend a lot of time at home, fixing it up and making look nice?

290. Do you like to be anywhere but at home on the weekends?

291. Would prefer to go to a ball game, a festival, or practically any other event rather than stay home to redecorate or renovate your home?

♥ ♥ ♥

Smoking

292. **Do you smoke?**

293. **Would you prefer that your partner not smoke?**

294. **Would you stop dating a person if that person had no intention of quitting smoking some time in the near future?**

295. **Do you think that smokers' hair, clothes, car, and homes often smell awful?**

296. **Do you think smokers who can't quit simply have no will power?**

297. **Do you think quitting smoking is extremely difficult?**

298. **Do you get angry when you are in a situation in which you must inhale others' cigarette smoke?**

If you are a smoker...

299. **Do you have any intention of quitting smoking?**

300. **As a smoker, do you get angry at non-smokers who think they are the only ones with rights?**

301. If you went to a friend's house for dinner and was asked not to smoke in the house, would you leave and not come back?

302. Do you try to be a considerate smoker and not smoke around people who object to it?

303. Would you like to quit smoking some time soon?

Drinking

304. Do you drink alcoholic beverages?

305. Have you ever sought help for a drinking problem?

306. Are you an alcoholic?

If you drink...

307. Would you like to stop drinking?

308. Do you drink socially? Explain what that means to you.

309. Do you drink only when you go out to a bar or restaurant?

310. Do you drink, but only on weekends?

311. Do you drink a little almost every day?

♥ ♥ ♥

312. When you go out to a bar, restaurant, or social gathering, do you usually have six or more alcoholic drinks?

313. When you go out to a bar, restaurant, or social gathering, do you rarely have more than two drinks?

314. If you drink, do you usually drink at home?

315. Do you usually have no more than two drinks a day when you drink at home?

316. Do you think it's no one's business how much you drink?

317. In the past, have you been arrested for driving while intoxicated or driving under the influence of alcohol?

318. Would you end our relationship if your partner was an alcoholic who refused to obtain help?

Drug Use

319. If offered marijuana at a party, would you smoke it?

320. If given an opportunity, would you purchase illegal drugs?

321. If you found your partner used illegal drugs, would you end the relationship?

322. If given an opportunity, would you try LSD, heroin, cocaine, or other drugs to see what all the fuss was about?

323. Do you think that taking illegal drugs are not worth the risk of getting arrested?

324. Should some drugs be legalized?

325. Do you take illegal drugs? Do you take any *legal* drugs?

326. Do any of your friends take drugs?

Emotional Health

327. Do you get angry very often?

328. If you get angry about something, do you try not to let it bother you?

329. When you get really angry, can people tell you are angry, or do you try to hide it?

330. Do you often get angry at the people you work for? Or at co-workers?

331. Have you been arrested before? If so, how many times?

332. Have you ever spent time in jail?

333. Have you ever been told you have a quick temper?

334. Have you ever hit someone before?

335. What would make you hit someone?

336. Have you ever destroyed objects during outbursts of anger?

337. How do you handle stress?

338. What would you do if your partner ever hit you? Would you end the relationship?

339. Do you think psychological therapy is beneficial? Have you ever been through therapy?

340. If your relationship with your partner was in trouble, would you seek professional counseling?

341. What would you do if your partner emotionally abused you?

342. Do you like to talk to your partner about your feelings?

♥ ♥ ♥

343. Have you been advised to take anti-depressant medication or other mood-altering drugs? Did you take that advice?

344. Do you need a little quiet time every day, all to yourself?

345. Do you resent your partner making decisions for you, no matter how well intentioned?

346. Do you believe in telling your partner when and where you are going and when you will return?

Thoughts on Body Weight

347. Do you think people are obsessed with their weight these days, and that as long as they are healthy, they should stop worrying?

348. Do you believe overweight people are unattractive?

349. Do you become angry when you hear people tell jokes ridiculing overweight people?

350. Do you believe that most overweight people don't try hard enough to lose weight?

♥ ♥ ♥

351. If your partner put on weight during your relationship, would that would be reason enough for you to end the relationship?

352. Do you regularly exercise to keep yourself in shape, and do you expect your partner to do the same?

353. Would you be embarrassed to be seen in public with an overweight person?

354. Do you think it is more difficult for women to lose weight than it is for men?

355. Do you find a little bit of extra weight on a person sexy?

Sex

356. Should a couple wait for marriage before becoming physically intimate?

357. Do you think too many people become too intimate too quickly?

358. How important do you think sex is in a relationship?

359. Are you comfortable talking about sex?

360. What are your thoughts on sex?

♥ ♥ ♥

361. What part of the day do you feel most sexy?

362. Would you continue a relationship in which there was no sex?

363. When women say "No," do they sometime mean "Yes?"

364. Is birth control the responsibility of the woman *and* the man?

365. Do you think that these days it is absolutely necessary to use condoms, regardless of how "nice" the person seems?

366. Would you ever be so foolish as to make love without using a condom?

367. For men: If a woman is not using some form of birth control, and you are ready to make love, do you think that's her problem?

368. If a person does not enjoy making love, do you want a relationship with that person?

369. Is it a good idea to talk about sex with your partner?

370. How many times a month do you think it is normal to make love?

371. Do you think a couple must be honest in sharing their thoughts about making love?

♥ ♥ ♥

372. If you and your partner were experiencing sexual dysfunction of any kind, would you hesitate to attend counseling sessions with your partner?

373. If your partner had been exposed to AIDS, would you expect your partner to tell you immediately? And would you do the same?

374. If you found you had been exposed to any sexually transmitted disease, would you immediately tell your partner, and would you expect your partner to do the same?

375. Do you have you a disease or condition that can be transmitted sexually?

376. Do you have a disease or condition that can be transmitted sexually that is now dormant and is not now contagious?

377. Do you insist on AIDS tests for yourself and your partner before you begin a sexual relationship with each other?

378. Do you have the AIDS virus?

379. Are you HIV Positive?

380. Have you been tested for the AIDS virus in the past?

♥ ♥ ♥

381. **Are you aware of all the ways that AIDS can be transmitted?** (Note: If the answer is "no," look at **http://www.safersex.org**)

382. **Are you aware of all the symptoms of other sexually transmitted diseases? Do you know there are sometimes no symptoms?** (See http://www.healthtouch.com/levell/leaflets/6349/6350.htm.)

383. **For men: If your partner became pregnant, do you believe the decision to continue the pregnancy would be her decision, and would you support whatever decision she made?**

384. **For women: If you became pregnant, do you think you would terminate the pregnancy?**

385. **Do you think abortion should remain legal?**

386. **Do you think it is extremely important for a man and woman to discuss birth control methods before having sex?**

387. **Do you agree with the statement: "There is no such thing as 100% safe sex"?**

388. **Do you realize that some sexually transmitted diseases can be transmitted even when a condom is used?**

♥ ♥ ♥

389. Do you think that people who have sexual fantasies are not normal?

390. Are sexual fantasies harmless?

391. Do you think discussing sexual fantasies enhances one's love life?

392. Would it bother you if your partner bought sexually oriented magazines, books, or videos?

Money

393. When two people date, should the man pay all expenses?

394. Should a married couple keep all expenses separate and determine who will pay for each expense? Or should they combine their money?

395. Should married couples have separate checking or savings accounts?

396. Should the husband or the wife handle the finances?

397. Should the husband and wife share responsibility and decision-making roles?

398. Should one spouse get an allowance and the other person handle the finances?

♥ ♥ ♥

399. Is a formal budget the best way to handle finances?

400. Do you balance your checkbook every month? Do you ever balance it?

401. Do you think it is okay to charge purchases up to the limit of the charge card and carry the balance month to month?

402. Do you think it's important to pay off balances each month on charge cards?

403. Is it important to save in order to enjoy things, such as vacation travel?

404. If you want to do something, such as take a trip, do you have any qualms about charging it to a credit card?

405. Do you save part of every paycheck?

406. If you were to marry, would you expect your spouse to sign a prenuptial agreement?

407. If you were to marry, and your spouse had large debts, would you agree to pay off those debts?

408. If you were to marry, would you expect your spouse to independently pay off any debts he or she incurred before our marriage?

409. If you were to marry, and your spouse bought more things than you both could afford, creating large debts, would you be very angry (because legally you would be responsible for those debts if they were charged to joint credit)?

410. If only one spouse is working (outside the home) in a marriage, do you think the working spouse should control where the money goes?

411. If you were married, and your spouse needed a new car, would you expect your spouse to pay for all of it if he/she were working?

412. If your spouse wanted to quit work to continue school full time, would you have any objection to supporting him/her?

413. If you wanted to quit work to continue schooling full time, would you expect your spouse to support you financially?

414. Do you think the spouse earning the higher income should make the major financial decisions?

415. Do you think the spouse earning the higher income should not be expected to handle as many of the household chores as the spouse with a lower income?

416. Do you think the spouse with the most important job is the person who earns the higher income?

417. Do you think the spouse who earns the higher income is often more physically exhausted at the end of the day than the spouse who earns the lower (or no) income?

418. If your spouse's relative(s) needed money (and could not afford to repay a loan), would you have any problem giving them money and not expect repayment?

419. If your spouse wanted to quit a good-paying job and take a lesser-paying job that he or she enjoyed more, would you object?

420. Do you think the best way to raise a family is for the wife to stay home full time to take care of the children and have the husband financially support the family?

421. Do you expect your spouse to work full time, whether or not you have children?

422. Is it important to have a will and to keep it up to date?

423. Is it important for a husband and wife to each have life insurance?

424. Do you think leaving a $5 tip on a $30 restaurant bill is too high a tip, even if the food and service were excellent?

425. If you were given a million dollars, what would be your first purchase?

If you've been previously married...

426. If you remarried, would you make up a new will leaving everything to your new spouse and leave nothing to your children?

427. If you remarried, would you make up a new will in which would you split your estate between your new spouse and your children?

Household Chores

428. Do you think that because everyone living in the house helps to make the house dirty, everyone should help clean it up?

429. Do you enjoy cleaning your home?

430. Do you enjoy repairing things around the house?

431. Do you dislike making household repairs, but you'd rather try to fix things yourself than have to pay someone to fix them?

432. Have you ever deliberately smashed something you were trying to repair because the repair was just not going right?

433. Does it drive you crazy to see someone throw clothes on the floor?

434. Is it important that you clean your home every day?

435. Do you think that because couples are so busy these days that the only sensible approach to cleaning the house is to hire someone else to do it?

436. Should a couple do yard work together?

437. Do messy homes make you uncomfortable?

438. Are washing and ironing clothes woman's work?

439. Do extremely clean homes make you uncomfortable?

Relatives

440. Do you like most of your relatives?

441. Do you think that just because someone is related to you, that is not enough reason to spend time with them?

442. If a parent causes an adult child too much pain, do you think the adult child should sever ties with that parent?

443. Do you think it doesn't matter what a relative does to you, that you should still respect all your relatives?

444. If your parent or an in-law became too involved in your personal affairs, would you cut that person out of your life?

445. Do you think it is important that the roles of in-laws be identified and agreed upon in the early stages of a marriage?

446. Do you think it is important for adult children to be emotionally and financially independent of their parents?

447. Do you believe parents and parents-in-law should never give advice unless their children ask for it?

448. Would you appreciate the advice of your parents or parents-in-law?

449. Would you mind having any one (or both) of your parents living with you and your partner if they needed to do so?

450. Would you mind having one (or both) of your in-laws living with you and your partner if they needed to do so?

451. Would you mind living with your parents or parents-in-law if you and your partner were having money problems?

452. Do you enjoy helping out your relatives?

453. Would you resent having to help your relatives?

454. Would you resent having to help out your spouse's relatives?

455. If your parents did not approve of your partner, what would you do?

456. Do you think it may not be a good idea to discuss your marital problems with your parents because they may hold a grudge against your partner once the problems are resolved?

457. Do you enjoy attending social gatherings of relatives?

458. During a social gathering of relatives, do you try to find a quiet corner to wait until it's time to go home?

♥ ♥ ♥

Children

459. Do you have children?

460. Did you have a happy childhood?

461. Do you want to have children in the future?

462. Would you consider adopting children?

463. If you and your partner had trouble conceiving a child, would you try every procedure available, no matter how involved or expensive, to help you have a baby?

464. Is changing diapers a woman's responsibility?

465. Do think there is anything wrong with spanking children?

466. Do you know what "shaken baby syndrome" is? (If not, see http://vh.radiology.uiowa.edu/Providers/ChildAbuse/PACA/html/ShakingShocker.html)

467. Do you think the father should be the one to discipline the children?

468. Do you think teenagers are not to be trusted?

469. If your teenage daughter became pregnant, would you kick her out of the house?

470. Do you enjoy children, no matter what age they are?

471. If your teenage son fathered a child, would you kick him out of the house?

472. If you married a person with children, would you mind playing the role of parent to those children?

473. Do you understand that children often experience problems in accepting a step-parent?

474. If you were a step-parent, would you expect to discipline the children?

475. If you married a person with grandchildren, would you mind playing the role of grandparent to those children?

476. In raising you, did your parents make some mistakes that you feel you will not repeat in raising your own children?

♥ ♥ ♥

477. If your partner physically or emotionally abused your child, or any child, would you end the relationship if your partner did not seek counseling to stop the abusive behavior?

478. If your partner sexually abused your child, or any child, would you end the relationship?

Travel

479. Would you like to travel around your state (or province)?

480. Would you like to travel around the country?

481. Would you like to travel to different parts of the world?

482. Would you like to move out of the city or town in which you currently live and live elsewhere in the state/province?

The Future

483. Would you like to move to another part of the country someday?

484. Would you like to retire soon?

485. Would you like to retire at an age younger than 65?

♥ ♥ ♥

486. Do you think that you will not retire because you will not be able to afford it?

487. Do you enjoy your work too much to retire?

488. If you had someone to support you, would you quit your job and stay home?

489. If you had someone to support you, would you quit your job and take a lower-paying, more personally satisfying job?

490. Someday, would you like to marry (or if previously married, marry again)?

491. Describe your perfect mate.

492. Would you like to continue your schooling?

493. Would you like to obtain a college degree in a field that is different from your current field?

494. Would you like to quit your current job and obtain another one?

495. Would you like to take some evening courses in subjects that interest you?

496. Would it bother you to be alone as you grow older?

497. Do you want to change your life? Explain.

498. What are the three most important things in life to you?

499. Were you 100% honest when you answered these questions?

500. Have you ever answered this many questions in your entire life?

Congratulations! Answering all those questions is an accomplishment. You should be proud of yourself. You now have a better understanding of your cyber-sweetie. You may have also experienced an extra benefit—you may have discovered a little bit about *yourself*!

In the next section, you'll read about shortcuts, smileys, and Internet vocabulary that will help you make sense of the wacky, wild, wonderful world of the Web.

♥ ♥ ♥

Smileys and Shortcuts

Smileys are "face" symbols that you need to move your head sideways to see. You can use these symbols to better express your intent. The most common ones are:

:-)	smile
:)	smile with no nose
:(	unhappy with no nose
>:-(	mad, annoyed
:-P	sticking out tongue
% {	hung over
**	When placed next to a name, it means the person typing is kissing that person [example: Stephen**]. When placed on either side of a word, it's used as quotes or used to emphasize the words. [example: I love ***Stephen***]
(( ))	This is a hug, and the name of the person being hugged is placed inside the parentheses. [For example: ((Steviebaby))]
(_)?	Have a cup of coffee.
@-->-->--	A rose

♥ ♥ ♥

Other Smileys

Of course, you can always come up with your own smileys. The possibilities are endless. Here are some examples:

><(((((:>	Something's fishy
(8- l >	You are bald with glasses and a beard.
(_)(_)	You are mooning someone, or you just have a big butt.
iiiiiiiii	It's your birthday and those are your birthday candles
%%%%	You just feel like typing percentages because they look nice.
^o-o^	You are a nerdy intellectual (or you like string bikini tops).
^v^	You are batty (or you like string bikini bottoms).
D	You're pregnant.
{{{{{{8-(	You have a headache.

♥ ♥ ♥

Shortcuts

So many phrases are repeatedly typed; you can save time and money (and delay carpal tunnel syndrome) by using shortcuts.

AOL	America Online
BAK	Back at keyboard
BTW	By the way.
BRB	Be right back.
f2f	Face to face
FWIW	For what it's worth
FYI	For your information
IMO	In my opinion
IMHO	In my humble opinion.
IRL	In real life
LOL	Laughing out loud
POV	Point of view
ROFLMAO	Rolling on the floor, laughing my derriere off.
ROFLAPMP	Rolling on the floor, voiding.
RTFM	Read the freakin' manual.
TIA	Thanks in advance.
TOS	On AOL, this means "Terms of Service." If you are threatened with being TOSd, it means you have violated the terms (by using vulgarity, for example), and you will be kicked off the system.

♥ ♥ ♥

Other Shortcuts

Of course, this language is just beginning, so there is room for improvement, and plenty of room for new shortcuts. Here are a few of mine that may be particularly useful for those slow typists among us. Create some yourself. Who knows, maybe someone will use them some time.

TU	Thank you.
HHD?	Hey, how ya doin'?
N2BD	Not too bad.
UMMC :)	You make me crazy (in a good way).
UCMU	You crack me up.
ICLU	I cyber-love you.
T1HAEZ	Typing one handed ain't easy.
JKYS!	Just kidding, you silly!
DBAA	Don't be an ass.
YRC	Y'all are crazy.
SMIDGIFTCSB	Sorry, mister, I don't go in for that cyber-sex baloney.
NINN	No, I'm not naked.
ITAP?	Is that a problem?
GAB	Gimme a break.
GGMMH	Gotta go, my mother's here.
GGMHH	Gotta go, my husband's here.
GGMWH	Gotta go, my wife's here.

GGS2M$	Gotta go. Spent too much money.
GGTIMC	Gotta go, this isn't my computer.
GGFIIDLN	Gonna get fired if I don't leave now.
GGP	Gotta go to the bathroom
2L84Me	Gotta go to sleep.

Internet Vocabulary For Impressing Your Friends

BBS
Bulletin Board System. Small online services that cater to a special interest.

browser
A software program that enables you to access Internet resources. Netscape, Mosaic, and Internet Explorer are examples of browsers.

cyber
A word often used in the media to preface just about anything having to do with the Internet. Web snobs abhor the word. I kind of cyberlike it.

FAQ
Documents containing Frequently Asked Questions about a particular subject. Often found in Usenet newsgroup archives. Developed because people were sick and tired of answering the same old questions. Always seek out FAQs before you bother people with a million questions.

flame
Short, nasty, email message.

FTP
File Transfer Protocol, a common method of moving files between two Internet sites.

Gopher　　A program that is linked to the Internet that helps people find files and other resources.

JPeG　　A file format used to transmit images over the Internet. GIF is another format. MPEG is a file format used to transmit video and sound.

IRC　　Internet Relay Chat. Similar to AOL chat rooms, but not as user friendly. But still fun. Available via the Internet.

lurking　　Watching, instead of taking part in, online discussions. Okay to lurk when you are a newbie.

mailing list　　A system that allows people to send email to one address; that message is then copied and sent to all subscribers of the list. Usually used to discuss one subject area.

modem　　Piece of hardware that allows transmission of digital information over telephone lines. It's actually a piece of 5" x 7" metal with a bunch of little wires and chips in it, and it's usually already installed inside newer computers.

Mosaic　　A browser that allows you to look at Internet resources.

Netscape　　A browser that allows you to look at Internet resources. Handles graphics and other features better than Mosaic.

newbie　　A person new to computers or to the Web

search engines　　Programs that allow you to enter title or content information on a particular subject, and the program searches the Web for related documents.

♥ ♥ ♥

surf   Another over-used word that Internet snobs dislike. Surfing the Web means that you continue to follow any links you find interesting. I like surfing.

Telnet   Enables users to interactively log on to a menu of services provided at Telnet sites.

thread   A series of mail messages in a discussion group that pertain to same topic.

tinysex   Another word for cybersex. You don't know what cybersex is? Well, to put it nicely, it's getting all hot and bothered with someone else online, usually in a private chat room.

URL   Universal Resource Locator. Also known as web site address. The following is an example of an URL: http://www.internet-romance.com/   (See next page for more info.)

Usenet   A world-wide system of discussion groups, called newsgroups.

Weboneer   A person who develops innovative ways to use the Internet. (Combination of Web and pioneer.) We are all Weboneers in a sense, as we stake our claim and settle into the Wild, Wild Web. (I made up "Weboneer." Feel free to use it any time.)

Basic URL Explanation

Example: http://www.online-romance.com

http://www: **http**: = **h**ypertext **t**ransfer **p**rotocol and it basically means: "To:" and **www** means world wide web.   A URL may also begin with ftp://, gopher://, or news://. These access other parts of the Internet.

online-romance The descriptive name of the web site.

.com indicates this is a commercial site. Others may be: edu (educational); gov (government); org (non-profit organization) or net (public network). There may also be a two-letter designation of origin, such as uk (United Kingdom), ca (Canada), au (Australia), or kr (South Korea). Sites from the U.S. have no two-letter country designation.

A slash (/) Indicates there are multiple pages at the site.

Note: Up to the end of the ".com/" designation, the URL is not case sensitive. After the ".com" it *is* case sensitive, so type the URL exactly as stated for best results.

♥ ♥ ♥

Resources

America Online	1-800-827-6364
CompuServe	1-800-848-8199
Prodigy	1-800-PRODIGY
AT&T	1-800-967-5363
Internet MCI	1-800-955-0927
Sprint	1800-877-4646
BBS Direct	1-800-939-4262
Microsoft	1-800-426-9400

Books About the Internet:

Go to your neighborhood bookstore. Go to shelf marked "Online" or "Computers." Close your eyes, turn around three times, click your heels, and then point. Open your eyes. Buy that one.

Magazines:

Wired, Internet World, Yahoo!

♥ ♥ ♥

Need A Book?

To order **The Little Book of Online Romance** or **The Original LOVERS'**
QUESTIONNAIRE Book, *A Fun Way To Compare Values*:

1. Go back to wherever you bought this one; or special order it at any bookstore OR
2. Call 1-800-828-6772 to charge it OR
3. Go to **http://www.amazon.com** and order it online OR
4. Send your check or money order, with your full address, to:

> LORMAX Communications
> PO Box 40304
> Raleigh, NC 27604

		Total
The Little Book of Online Romance	$6.95 plus $3 shipping/handling	US $9.95*
The Orig'l LOVERS' Questionnaire Book	$9.95 plus $4.75 shipping/handling	US $14.70*

*NC residents add 6%.

♥ ♥ ♥

The *Thank You* Page

♥

Thanks to: My husband, Stephen, for putting up with my eyeballs glued to a computer screen for many months and to my children for remembering they have a mother despite my hibernation, and to Cliff Schell, Nancy Kiplinger, and the PMA group for information and encouragement. Kisses to my sisters Susan Bates and Polly Barnett and all my friends and relatives in The Frozen North, you know who you are. (Get on email so we can talk!) Hugs to Sandy Allaire, Pam & Bob Dolan, Jeff Halter, Lois Tipton & Simon Pontin, all wired and wonderful. Hugs, too, to Susan Gibson and Jan Wallace. Thanks to: Guy McCool, Michael Gutierrez-May, Sam Favate, Alex Vinogradov, THopeB, Phylwriter, TwisterB, Margaret Moseley, Ron Burris, Katherine Harris, Laura and Kris Neely, Rene Bartlett and Robert Montgomery, Paula Guran, Colleen; and Laurie Kilmartin for making me laugh online and off, and *all the friendly folks in my favorite chat room.* Thanks, too, to Mike and Angel Williamson; Michael Bennett, a talented graphic designer/illustrator; Great Impressions, a Dallas printer with an appropriate name; and Nancy Goodyear. And thanks to Oprah Winfrey, for your entertaining, inspiring, insightful, and educational shows and for hiring HarpoLiz. (So I'm addicted to Oprah and the Internet. Is that a problem? ;)) And of course, thanks to Molly, Foxy, and Sampson for your ever-present canine grins. (I know dogs can't read. I'll read it to them.)

♥

Keep Track of CyberFriends:

Screen Name	Location	Identifying Info	Discussion Topics

♥ ♥ ♥

Keep Track of CyberFriends:

Email Address	Location	Identifying Info	Discussion Topics

Keep Track of CyberFriends:

Email Address	Location	Identifying Info	Discussion Topics

♥ ♥ ♥

Keep Track of CyberFriends:

Screen Name	Location	Identifying Info	Discussion Topics

Keep Track of CyberFriends:

Screen Name	Location	Identifying Info	Discussion Topics

Keep Track of CyberFriends:

Screen Name	Location	Identifying Info	Discussion Topics

♥ ♥ ♥

Keep Track of CyberFriends:

Screen Name	Location	Identifying Info	Discussion Topics

Keep Track of CyberFriends:

Screen Name	Location	Identifying Info	Discussion Topics

Keep Track of CyberFriends:

Screen Name	Location	Identifying Info	Discussion Topics

♥ ♥ ♥

About The Author

In addition to her book career, **Lorilyn Bailey** is an instructional designer for a software company and develops Web-based training materials. Her career adventures include several years as a technical training consultant, an (award-winning) PBS writer/features producer, and a personnel coordinator. Other interests include psychology, humor, Victoriana, and travel.

Ms. Bailey holds a B.A. degree in Communications/ Journalism from St. John Fisher College and has nearly completed an M.S. degree in Instructional Technology from Rochester Institute of Technology.

Her first book, **<u>The Original LOVERS' QUESTIONNAIRE Book</u>**, is highly recommended by counselors and psychologists, including Barbara DeAngelis, PhD, (author of <u>Real Moments</u> and <u>Are You The One For Me?,</u>) who calls it, "*A valuable tool to help you discover if your partner is the right one for you.*"   Ms. Bailey lives in North Carolina with her family. She invites you to visit her website at **http://www.online-romance.com.**